PERFORM.

The Unsexy Truth about (Startup) Success

Written by Stoyan Yankov and Cristobal Alonso

Language editing by Jessica Sandin
Design and Illustrations by Agnė Štrimaitytė

What Readers Say

"This is a must-read book for any entrepreneur to get an overview of the tools they can use to turn their idea into a successful sustainable business. While the book is primarily targeting young entrepreneurs, I find it to be useful for the experienced and successful ones as well. I am myself planning to apply a few of the tools in the book right away, and I will definitely recommend my team to read PERFORM."
- Justas Janauskas, CEO Qoorio, former Founder & CEO at Vinted

"An early focus on defining and implementing a strong workplace culture is an effort you can't overlook. PERFORM nails it on the head with strong examples of startups doing this right and gives you an easy to follow format to do it yourself."
- David Bizer, Founder & CEO at Talent Fountain and former First Recruiter at Google Europe

"For my company, I have ordered 10 more copies of this book and will distribute them among the team, because there are tons of learnings which can be applied!"
- Chris Robbins, CEO at Tele2 Estonia

"I wish I could read this book at least 10 years ago, but you can do it just now!"
- Liudas Kanapienis, Co-Founder & CEO of OnDato

"Great book! It's an operating system not only for startups but also for innovation and product teams inside corporates. Thank you!"
- Luis Villa del Campo, Principal Director - Growth & Strategy Europe at Accenture

"I read a lot of business books, and in many of them you can find the same examples repeating over and over again. However, this book is very actionable, it is a fast-read, has great illustrations and practical approach."
- Tim Hall, Co-founder & CEO at Simporter

"This book is MUST for every ambitious entrepreneur!"
- Peter Sandberg, Founding Partner at Nordic Secondary Fund

"It is always great to read the stories and learn from others. And the #PERFORM book is a huge selection of such stories from successful European businesses."
- Ilma Nausedaite, Co-founder & COO at MailerLite

"I feel inspired by the book to do some changes in our own startup. Changes that I believe will help us to succeed in "the jungle". Thank you for the mind-opening book!"
- Tanya Kostadinova, Co-founder at Canap Foods

"I definitely recommend reading the book because it contains great pieces of advice. It can really help you to take control of your time and be more efficient as a founder."
- Anna Stepanoff, Founder & CEO at WildCodeSchool

"Great book! Focused, pragmatic and to the point, easy to read. I recommend it."
- Fernando Molina, Managing Partner at 5G Ventures

"This is a must-buy book! If you are an entrepreneur, this book is the answer."
- James Arthur Williams, Associate Professor at University of Tennessee

"This book has a potential to become like a manual that you take and re-read from time to time instead of reading it once and putting it on a shelf."
- Roberts Bernans, Co-founder & CPO at Nordigens

"This book is a treasure for every entrepreneur or anyone who would like to start a business from scratch, and shows how to master the most important challenges in the startup and as an individual."
- Erich Althaus, CEO at noline.ch

"One of the hottest book releases of #2020. There are brilliant concepts and methods that can be used by any team in any organization, and also individually. Generations of entrepreneurs will feel the same after reading it!"
- Razvan Suta, Co-founder and COO at polisens.io

"It's great timing for such a book since all entrepreneurs went through many unexpected challenges in 2020."
- Alexander Zlatkov, Co-Founder & CEO at SessionStack

"I've recently finished reading the book and am so inspired. It's full of stories and advice every founder can benefit from."
- Viktoriya Vasilenko, Founder & CEO at Knowledge Gate Group

"This is an incredibly valuable piece, I enjoyed it so much - easy to read, highly practical and a great support on the startup journey!"
- Annija Matisone, Co-founder at The Leaders Who Care

"Well-organised handbook for the first-time entrepreneurs, as well as valuable reading for professionals to keep the discipline. Includes practical advice, tangible and realistic examples."
- Davids Stebelis, Partner & Board Member at ALINA SIA

"That's just a must-read book if you are considering building your own startup."
- Marija Gracova, Student at The Stockholm School of Economics

"I think it's a great book for both, new and also experienced founders. A very good read!"
- Maris Dagis, Founder & CEO of Sellfy

"I really enjoyed how easy and straightforward it was to read, at the same time being full with no BS, on-the-point examples and good references."
- Janis Putnins, Founder at Flipful

"Awesome read! Thanks for crafting this masterpiece!"
- German Silos, Founder & CEO at Instituto Psicológico Cláritas

Contents

Preface

Our journey to the PERFORM Methodology and this book

We met in 2016. Cristobal remembers the moment vividly. At the time, Cristobal and his team at startup accelerator Startup Wise Guys (SWG) were driving a program across Denmark for Telia, the telecoms provider. The SWG team was listening to startup pitches, giving them feedback and recruiting startups for what was going to be one of Denmark's largest onsite hackathons to date: JUMP. SWG had just finished giving tough feedback to some of the startups in Aarhus, a coastal city, when a passionate Bulgarian guy came to talk to Cristobal.

Stoyan had lived in Denmark for a number of years. He was an ambitious guy, who had worked hard to become a reputable movie producer and was running his own video production company. But he didn't want to do it anymore. Inspired by Tony Robbins and other motivational speakers, he wanted to become one of them: a speaker inspiring people around the world to take ownership of their path and design a happy and productive life.

The journey ahead wouldn't be easy. It's difficult to build your name from a scratch, particularly if you're from Eastern Europe. But Stoyan was driven by a strong inner purpose and ready to endure the journey. He slept in his client's office when he was giving workshops to reduce travelling time and expenses. He took a part-time job as a dishwasher at a restaurant to get some cash while building his client base. He would listen to podcasts and audiobooks while washing dishes. He wanted to keep learning. He wanted to find and craft his message, decide which angle to take and whom to serve.

Speaking to Cristobal, Stoyan shared his plans to become a globally known speaker, mentioning his initial talk, Life is like a movie. Cristobal saw passion in his eyes and thought: "Why not?". Cristobal told Stoyan that SWG always supports entrepreneurs. He suggested that Stoyan come give his talk to some of SWG's startups. At the time, SWG had a batch of startups in Riga, Latvia[1]. By speaking to them, Stoyan could get feedback from the startups and Cristobal's team and start building his profile. Cristobal remembers listening to Stoyan's talk and getting inspired by the short meditation at the end. Ever since, when delivering workshops together, it's our signature piece - The Grand Finale. It's an inspiring moment for everyone.

Stoyan had purpose and believed 110% in what he wanted to achieve. That drove him to do whatever it takes to get there. He has now delivered hundreds of keynotes and workshops in more than 25 countries. In the meantime, he has continued coaching SWG batches. His workshops and one-to-one sessions are always rated highly and get great feedback from the startups.

At the beginning of 2019, we managed to catch up in Copenhagen after we'd both been busy travelling. At the time, we were both thinking about writing our own books. Cristobal regularly coached startups on culture, values and planning and wanted to put the material into a book. Stoyan was planning to write a book about productivity and performance and had just been running his PERFORM MVP[2] workshops. It made a lot of sense to join forces. The PERFORM methodology was born.

Together, we developed the content and during 2019 we introduced the PERFORM methodology in keynotes at tech- and startup conferences. We tested the content several times in workshops for SWG batches, with other international accelerators and by coaching startup teams. We also took the framework to SMEs[3], professional service firms and larger companies. We got very encouraging feedback. The material really resonated with people. We decided it was time to write this book and to continue chasing our dreams and passions.

We've written this book for you, the founder. We want to increase

---

1   Startup Wise Guys Batch 7 in Riga, where SWG had invested in 8 startups. They spent four months full-time with SWG accelerating their ventures.
2   Minimum Viable Product.
3   Small and Medium-Sized Enterprises.

your chance of success. If you're willing to focus on the unsexy side of running a startup, you'll reap the rewards.

We made another important decision: to base most of the examples we'll be sharing with you on startups from the NewEurope region, our home base. We'll explain why:

NewEurope: A thriving, dynamic startup region that's too often ignored

More and more unicorns from the Baltics, Central Eastern Europe (CEE) and the Commonwealth of Independent States (CIS) are making the headlines these days - think of TransferWise, Grammarly, Vinted, UiPath and many more. However, there is neither much literature nor research about the region. Throughout this book, we'll refer to this region as NewEurope.

What makes this region different and special?

We have witnessed one phenomenon repeatedly. At SWG, we bring a group of Angel investors from the Nordics or Western Europe to the events where we select startups to invest in. Without exception, these Angels get overwhelmed and excited. They tell us that the level of passion, energy, ambition and determination they find among these startup founders far surpasses what they encounter in entrepreneurs back home, whether that's Denmark, Norway, Germany or somewhere else. What makes these entrepreneurs - young and not so young, from many different countries in NewEurope - so special?

Most of the countries in NewEurope became independent or left the communist block in the early 1990s. Many of the entrepreneurs making the headlines now are from the first generation to have lived their entire adult lives within a capitalist system. Their parents built the countries with their own hands, fuelled by their own ideas.

Typically, there are not yet any role models for entrepreneurs. The founders are themselves giving others advice while making their own startups work. They are willing to take risks and to go the extra mile.

They're not afraid of having a lower standard of living for a few years and they have no real fear of failure. They only worry about not being tough enough or good enough - that would dent their pride. Their domestic markets are never their end objective. They are international from the start: global, ambitious and full of desire to make it. This combination of ingredients - eagerness, ambition, a global outlook, tech knowledge and frugality - creates a mix that is ready to thrill.

This is why we love NewEurope. This is why we believe this region will produce more great international tech companies than Western Europe in the coming decade, while requiring less than 20% of the investment that would be needed in the West. As an example, the Baltics, with less than six million inhabitants across its three countries (Estonia, Latvia and Lithuania) has already produced six unicorns (Skype[4], Transferwise, Pipedrive, Playtech, Bolt and Vinted), has the highest amount of startup funding per capita[5] and the highest number of startups per capita in Europe. According to the World Bank Global Entrepreneurship Monitor[6], Latvia (the only Baltic country included) and the Slovak Republic are second and third only to Armenia in a comparison of the total early-stage entrepreneurial activity rate in Europe. The share of adults involved in entrepreneurship in these markets is double or even triple the rates in Spain, Sweden, the UK or Germany. Imagine the outcomes as these rates of entrepreneurship spread to much larger countries in NewEurope, such as Poland, Romania, Ukraine or Turkey. In these countries, where entrepreneurship was suppressed, people are turning to the Baltics as the example to follow, rather than Silicon Valley or the UK.

A few notes before you get into the book

NewEurope presents a tremendous opportunity, whether you are looking to invest in or learn from this new generation of entrepreneurs. We have been fortunate to be able to leverage our personal networks

---

4   Skype was created by Swede Niklas Zennström and Dane Janus Friis, in cooperation with Ahti Heinla, Priit Kasesalu, Jaan Tallinn and Toivo Annus, Estonians who developed the peer-to-peer backend that was also used in the music-sharing application Kazaa. Skype is, therefore, referred to as Estonia's first unicorn.
5   Baltic Startup Scene Report 2018-2019.
6   Percentage of adults: Armenia 21%, Latvia 15.4%, Slovakia 13.3%. Source: World Bank Global Entrepreneurship Monitor 2019.

and the SWG family to get amazing tips, personal and founder stories for this book. We believe these examples will resonate with you. You'll see the friends and contacts we've interviewed referred to by their first names.

Just like a startup, this book is a team effort between co-authors Cristobal and Stoyan. But, as we'll explain, to PERFORM, it's fundamental to have clear roles and responsibilities. Early on in the journey, we divided the chapters between us, but since we both feel strongly about every chapter, we use the plural "we" throughout the book. When referring to our individual experience, we use third person - either Cristobal or Stoyan. Last but not least, we love using examples from Startup Wise Guys (SWG) and its 220+ portfolio[7] experience.

Enjoy the book and let's start PERFORMing!

---

7   Size of the portfolio as of December 2020.

The PERFORM methodology

IN THIS CHAPTER, YOU WILL LEARN ABOUT:

» What the PERFORM methodology will do for you
» The seven components of PERFORM
» The benefits of mastering PERFORM for you and your company

"THE EVERYDAY LIFE OF AN ENTREPRENEUR IS DIGGING A MUDDY TRENCH. THERE'S LITTLE, VERY LITTLE GLAMOR. THREE THINGS ARE ESSENTIAL:

1. DIG FURTHER EVERY DAY.
2. RISE UP FOR A HELICOPTER VIEW EVERY MONTH.
3. CELEBRATE EVERY SUCCESS, EVERY TIME.

AND THEN, ONE CAN MOVE AHEAD AND GRACIOUSLY BEAR ALL THE BLOOD, SWEAT AND SORROW."

- Sergiu Negut, Co-founder and EVP, FintechOS[8]

---

8   FintechOS is a TaaS (Technology as a Service) company on a mission to change the way people experience and engage with financial technology, recognised by The Europas as 2020's Hottest Fintech Startup in Europe.

As an entrepreneur, you live in the jungle. Your main goal is to survive every day. In the jungle, you need to find food and water, to keep safe from dangerous animals and find shelter at the end of the day. The daily startup experience is often similar. You focus on keeping your head above water, with enough cash flow to cover your costs. The problem is that surviving for the sake of it might keep your startup going, but what's the point if it's going nowhere?

The odds are against us - entrepreneurs. You have probably seen the statistics showing that nine out of ten startups fail over time, many of them within the first two years. This is a hard and bleak truth, but one that you'd do well to consider. Cold statistics like these are not intended to discourage entrepreneurs, but to encourage us to work smarter and harder.

Being a visionary and a creative person is your biggest asset but can also be your biggest enemy. You need to PERFORM every day and every hour. You can't be a successful startup founder without being extremely efficient, having ruthless self-discipline and doing lots of planning.

We want to show you how to increase your startup's chances of survival to 50%, instead of only 10%[9]. Let's be clear: we're not proposing a magic potion. In fact, you probably already know what you have to do: work hard and be smart about it. The problem is that many founders simply don't do it. They don't do what it takes. They only want to do the fun and sexy stuff. That's why so many startups fail. If you pay attention to the ones that make it, you'll see that they are masters of PERFORM.

The PERFORM framework helps you consistently perform at your best as a team. If you consistently apply the seven areas of the framework, you will be way ahead of the majority of startups. Our experience with hundreds of startups shows that if you run your company well, your chance of success is 50%. Those are very good odds, worth betting your energy and passion on. If you are willing to focus on the unsexy side of running a startup, you'll dramatically increase your chance of success.

9   Startup Genome. The Global Startup Ecosystem Report 2020 (GSER2020), 2020. Retrieved from: https://startupgenome.com/reports/gser2020

The seven elements of PERFORM
P for Purpose & Values

P urpose & values

E ffective planning

R oles & responsibilities

F ocus & execution

O ptimal energy

R obust communication

M ental toughness

When a company has a strong **Why (Purpose)**, a clear and compelling **What (Vision)** and it operates with a clear **How (Values)**, it develops a powerful working culture. As an entrepreneur, you need to discuss these three elements from the get-go and let them guide you when making every important decision.

"YOUR PURPOSE IS THE WIND IN YOUR SAIL. AND WITHOUT A WHY THERE IS NO WIND"

– David Hieatt, Author of Do Purpose: Why Brands with a Purpose Do Better and Matter More[10]

---

10   Source: Hieatt, D. The quote retrieved from: https://leapcoaching.ie/inspirational-quotes/

E for Effective Planning

Planning gives you the ability to bring the future into the present. Once you know the company you want to create, you need a plan for how to get there. As a startup, your resources will be limited for a long time. Planning will give you perspective. It allows you to see the bigger picture and make smart and effective choices. You'll be effective and productive when you focus on getting the right things done and know what not to do.

"THERE IS NOTHING SO USELESS AS DOING EFFICIENTLY THAT WHICH SHOULD NOT BE DONE AT ALL[11]"

- Peter Drucker, Management guru

R for Roles and Responsibilities

Once you have planned what needs to be done, the question is who will do what: Who is responsible for which tasks. What each person takes on will depend on their role. In our experience, most founders don't define responsibilities properly. In reality, it needs to be done not just once but repeatedly, since responsibilities are bound to change as your company develops. Your team needs to review and revise responsibilities as roles evolve. By combining clearly defined responsibilities with the accountability of setting and meeting deadlines, you have a much greater chance of surviving and thriving.

---

11   Source: Drucker, P. Managing for Business Effectiveness, Harvard Business Review, 1963. Retrieved from:https://hbr.org/1963/05/managing-for-business-effectiveness

"BEING IN A FAST-GROWTH ORGANISATION DOESN'T MEAN YOU SHOULD BE FAST AND LOOSEN UP ROLES AND ACCOUNTABILITY. OUR GREATEST ASSET IS TIME, AND HAVING CLEAR ROLES, EXPECTATIONS, AND ACCOUNTABILITY HELPS US USE IT MORE EFFICIENTLY."

– Dillon Hall, Co-founder and CEO, Europe, Simporter

F for Focus & Execution

You know what you have to do, but can you execute? Can you get rid of the distractions that try to divert your attention every other second? We'll share some tools to help you improve your focus: use the ones that work for you. Focus will transform long hours of work into the right results. Move the needle by working **on** the business and not only **in** the business. What are you going to do with your ability to focus? You're going to Execute! We're not talking about being busy, but about relentless execution, on a massive scale.

The best decision is the fast decision. Cristobal loves to say: "Execution eats strategy for breakfast. Take 10 decisions fast, 3 of them are going to be wrong. So what? You go and fix them. But don't stay and overthink. You need to be ready to execute and get s**t done!"

"THE MAIN THING IS TO KEEP THE MAIN THING THE MAIN THING[12]."

- Steven Covey, keynote speaker and author of The 7 Habits of Highly Effective People

O for Optimal Energy

You're focused and you're turning your startup into an execution machine, but make sure you remember that building a successful startup might take you seven to ten years. That's a lot of time! It's more like a marathon than a sprint. We keep wondering why so many founders treat it as a sprint. If you want to build a winning team, you need to create a culture where you manage your own and your team's energy. It's all about building the right habits: sleeping, eating, hydrating, exercising and practicing mindfulness.

It's not just about mastering these habits. It's about creating a culture in your team where prioritizing energy is non-negotiable.

"TAKE CARE OF YOUR BODY. IT'S THE ONLY PLACE YOU HAVE TO LIVE[13]."

- Jim Rohn, Personal development guru

12   Source: Covey, S. Stephen Covey Quotes. BrainyQuote.com, n.d. Retrieved from: https://www.brainyquote.com/quotes/stephen_covey_110198

13   Source: Rohn, J. Jim Rohn Quotes. BrainyQuote.com, n.d. Retrieved from: https://www.brainyquote.com/quotes/jim_rohn_147499

R for Robust Communication

You and your company are running a ten-year startup marathon. To make sure your company runs well, it's fundamental to communicate well and consistently, across all parts of the organization. To make communication robust, incorporate both giving and receiving feedback into your culture. We know it's not easy, but every single minute you invest in feedback has payback. Feedback starts with you: as a leader, you need to give and listen to feedback. Develop systems and processes so that your managers can provide and receive feedback, too. It's your job to help them discover how powerful it can be.

"IN TEAMWORK, SILENCE ISN'T GOLDEN, IT'S DEADLY."

- Mark Sanborn[14], author, professional speaker and entrepreneur.

M for Mental Toughness

Even if you master communication and feedback across your company, there will be tough times ahead for any entrepreneur or founder. If you want to survive those periods and win, arm yourself with the mindset of a winning player. Master the mental game! You will need to develop the ability to deal with stressors and threats. That means minimizing the time you spend in a negative or victim mindset. Focus on the solution and on the result. Keep taking action, readjusting and refining your strategies. Don't stop until you achieve your goal.

"SUCCESS IS LIKE WRESTLING

---

14   Best-selling author and leadership speaker. In 2019, just published his latest book "The Intention Imperative: 3 Essential Changes That Will Make You a Successful Leader Today!"

WITH A GORILLA. YOU DON'T QUIT WHEN YOU'RE TIRED.
YOU QUIT WHEN THE GORILLA IS TIRED."[15]

- Robert Schwarz Strauss, American Politician and Diplomat

Now let's get into the details that will help you PERFORM.

15   Source: The article by Popik, B. The Big Apple, 2018, retrieved from https://www.barrypopik.com/index.php/
new_york_city/entry/training_is_like_wrestling
The quote by Strauss, R. S. said in December 1974 in the Washington (DC) Star-News.

PURPOSE & VALUES

IN THIS CHAPTER, YOU WILL LEARN ABOUT:

» The building blocks of a strong startup culture: Purpose (**Why**), Vision (**What**), and Values (**How**)
» The importance and benefits of a strong culture
» Values alignment as the key element when choosing co-founders
» When to start defining your startup culture and values
» Embracing and living your startup culture
» Exercises to help discuss and define purpose, vision, and values

"VERY FEW PEOPLE OR COMPANIES CAN CLEARLY ARTICULATE WHY THEY DO WHAT THEY DO. BY WHY I MEAN YOUR PURPOSE, YOUR CAUSE OR BELIEF: WHY DOES YOUR COMPANY EXIST? WHY DO YOU GET OUT OF BED IN THE MORNING? AND WHY SHOULD ANYONE CARE?"[16]

- Simon Sinek, Bestselling author and Leadership Consultant

16 Source: Sinek, S. Start with Why, Portfolio, 2009.

Purpose, vision and values for startups

Purpose
The reason for which something is done or created or for which something exists.

Values
Operating philosophy or principles that guide an organization's internal conduct as well as its relationships with customers, partners and shareholders.

In this chapter, we'll address a company's purpose, vision and values. These may seem like ambitious concepts for a new company, but we believe they are essential for success.

Until the start of the past decade, these concepts were typically not seen as important for startups. Today, early-stage companies realise they have value both for team building and for their overall business. Simon Sinek, with his TEDx talk[17] and the book *Start with Why*, was a driving force behind this. The rise in popularity of Sinek's theories had a profound impact on the startup ecosystem. Everyone started paying attention to the **Why**, including venture capitalists. Defining your purpose became part of the startup agenda.

To explore these concepts further, we first need to define them. The **purpose** of an organisation is the fundamental reason why the organisation exists[18]. It's Sinek's **Why**. Most corporations do a terrible job of living their purpose and connecting it to their employees' work. A study by PwC's strategy consulting business found that only a quarter of more than 500 people interviewed felt connected to their company's purpose[19].

---

17 Source: Sinek S. Start with Why - how great leaders inspire action, TEDxPugetSound, May 2014.
18 Source: Margolis, S. Purpose of an organization. Workplace Culture Institute, 2020. Retrieved from: https://sheilamargolis.com/core-culture-and-five-ps/the-five-ps-and-organizational-alignment/purpose/
19 Source: Study quoted in Blount, S., & Leinwand, P.. Why are we Here, Harvard Business Review, November 2019.

While the purpose asks **Why**, it is not a question addressing the products a company produces, but rather the change it wants to bring to its customers. A few examples of to illustrate this point:

» **Peak Games**[20], a mobile gaming company which was the first unicorn in Turkey and was recently acquired by Zynga, has the purpose "to provide products that enrich the lives of our users."
» **Pipedrive,** one of Estonia's unicorns and among the world's largest Software as a Service (SaaS) platforms for customer relationship management (CRM), with more than 95,000 customers. Its purpose is "To make sales success not only possible, but inevitable for teams everywhere."
» Not a big startup name, but an inspiring purpose from **Talium,** the Danish accountancy firm Stoyan uses, and its CEO Claus Fraussing Nielsen: "Helping small business owners sleep better at night."

For most companies, the purpose shouldn't change. The reason **Why** you do what you do will be constant, while **What** and **How** are both likely to evolve. The words used to define the purpose may be updated, refreshed or made more precise. However, the company's core purpose should be set for the long term. Only a radical change in company direction or ownership can change it.

The **vision** focuses on **What** a company plans to do, as well as helping to define what it will **not** do. Your vision is your north star, providing direction and helping the team make strategic decisions. For example, **TransferGo**[21], a well-known Lithuanian fintech company with more than 1.8 million users, is driven by the vision "to provide a simple and unified solution for consumer finance in a complex and global society, by scaling our international money transfer proposition globally [...]."

In a column on Inc.com[22], Benjamin Hardy uses a fitting analogy to help us see the value of a clear vision:

Consider a flight. The pilot of the airplane needs to reach a clearly

---

20 More information about the company can be found at: https://techcrunch.com/2020/06/01/zynga-acquires-turkeys-peak-games-for-1-8b-after-buying-its-card-games-studio-for-100m-in-2017/
21 TransferGo currently has more than 1.8 million customers. It is the second-largest fintech company to emerge from the Baltics in the past decade (after TransferWise) and was recently the best-rated money transfer company in the world (Trustpilot). The company is registered in the UK but the majority of its team and founders are based in Lithuania.
22 Source: B. Hardy, If you're too busy for these 5 things, your life is more off-course than you think, Inc.com, 8 Aug. 2017, https://www.inc.com/benjamin-p-hardy/if-youre-too-busy-for-these-5-things-your-life-is-.html

defined destination and has a flight plan. Did you know that due to unexpected circumstances (turbulence, weather conditions and other factors), airplanes are off course more than 90% of the flight time? The reason why they still reach their destination is simple: through air traffic control and the inertial guidance system[23], pilots are constantly correcting the course[24]. It's not hard for them to make these small corrections as they go, but if they fail to do so, the result can be catastrophic.

The same applies to startups. Even if you have a clear vision of where you're going, you will be hit by changes in the market, problems with customers, or internal issues with employees. When you know where you want to get to, you can adjust to the changes and correct your course towards the destination: your purpose. You can't control all events, nor predict all the circumstances. But you have the power to stay focused on your vision. When the airplane of your startup gets off track, you can navigate it back on course.

The power of an inspiring Vision: Curify

Curify, originally from Ukraine, is one of SWG's portfolio companies in the health sector. Initially, the founders told SWG they were building bots to improve the health industry. Being another 'bot-builder' is not going to inspire anyone, so we challenged them to think differently.
Their vision now is "A world with zero diseases." They believe there is no reason for an incurable disease to exist in the near future.
Curify doesn't expect to cure the world, but the founders believe they will contribute a small but crucial part to making it happen. The company aims to create the world's largest community for anyone interested in clinical research. This will solve the problem of patient recruitment for clinical trials by

---

23   An inertial navigation system is a navigation device that uses a computer, motion sensors and rotation sensors to continuously calculate by dead reckoning the position, the orientation, and the velocity of a moving object without the need for external references.
24   Applies to times when the autopilot system is not being used.

giving researchers instant access to patients interested in participating.

Rather than solving a medical problem, they are addressing a broken part of the process with a solution that could have a huge impact. The fast-tracking of activity tackling Covid-19 shows that it's possible to tackle the issues in drug development when there's a will to do so.

Values stand for **How**. It's an operating philosophy or principles that guide an organization's internal conduct as well as its relationships with customers, partners and shareholders. Values are fundamental to a company's culture and represent the core beliefs around which culture develops[25]. They guide each individual within an organization in their decision-making process. You may think about values as your operating system. It takes a while to shape them and make them work efficiently, but they are the crucial mechanism underlying everything once they work well.

Startup Wise Guys Organizational Values

OUR VALUES - WHAT WE BELIEVE IN:

WE ARE
FOUNDERS DRIVEN

SWG was built to help founders become entrepreneurs and we are true to this mission! We care deeply for the success of the founders we work with. In good times and tough times – we are on their side. Even being an investor, we keep the "founders' hat" always on.

WE ARE IN IT FOR
THE LONG-TERM

Not only are we in a long-term business, we also apply a long-term mindset. We are early believers and important catalyzers for both startups and ecosystems. It is a great responsibility which we carry with pride leading to long-lasting and strong impact.

WE ARE
PASSIONATE &
AMBITIOUS

We do not work at SWG because we have to, but because we want to. We dream big and we are ready to go the hard way to achieve our goals. Being passionate about startups and our jobs, gives us energy to push with persistency and get sh*t done. Being experienced and serious about what we do, makes us deliver the best.

WE ARE
ARE COMMUNITY AND
RELATIONSHIP BUILDERS,
THUS THE SWG FAMILY

We develop strong long-lasting communities and caring relationships – be it among startups or wider with mentors and investors. We spark friendships and collaboration rather than competition. The "SWG Family" is a tribe of like-minded and passionate people from all over the world. It is based on common values of trust, openness, respect, appreciation and two way support.

startupwiseguys.com

25   Source: Purtle, J. Defining Your Startup's Core Values - What Every Founder Should Know From Day One. Foundr, 2018. Retrieved from: https://foundr.com/define-core-values

The SWG values heavily influence our decisions. For example, one of our values is **"We are in it for the long term."** When a short-term engagement with a particular partner is not profitable, we still consider the potential of a long-term relationship building. More painfully, if we receive a profitable offer to collaborate from a potential partner who is not aligned with our values, we pass on it. Later in this chapter, we'll show you how we defined our values.

Focus on simple and memorable values: WildCodeSchool

Anna Stepanoff is the founder and CEO of WildCodeSchool, a company training web developers hands-on IT skills in more than 19 schools across Europe. WildCodeSchool has three simple values: Passion, Innovation and Humanity, but shaping them was a journey. "It took a couple of years and a number of workshops to finally be happy with them," Anna says.

They started with a much longer list. "But we realized that more than 3 is hard to remember," explains Anna. To her, that meant the initial long-list had to be simplified. "I believe everything about values and culture should be memorable." she notes. "So when you define yours, try to use easy to remember words and phrases. In our case, we even added a visual to each value and connected three behaviours that clarify what it means to live that value. That way it is easier for everyone from the team to understand what we stand for."

These three concepts - purpose, vision and values - are what sets the foundation for a successful startup. When a company has a definite purpose (**Why**), a clear and compelling vision (**What**) and firmly rooted values (**How**), they typically create an attractive company culture.

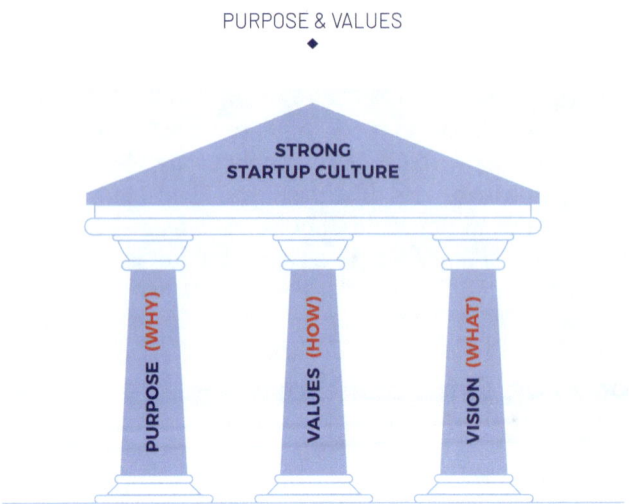

THE 3 PILLARS OF STRONG STARTUP CULTURE

Defining culture

Culture is a flexible set of norms; a subconsciously agreed framework for how things are done. Whether you define your vision and values or not, a culture will inevitably emerge through the people in your organization and how they act. The culture will evolve as the company grows, developing as the team develops. It's essential to know what kind of company culture you want, take responsibility for building it and guide it where you want it to go.

"CULTURE IS THE COLLECTION OF PEOPLE. YOU'VE GOT 130 PEOPLE OUT THERE MAKING DECISIONS EVERY DAY.

THOUSANDS OF DECISIONS ARE MADE EVERY DAY. CULTURE IS HOW YOU, AS… LEADER OF THE COMPANY, ARE CONFIDENT THAT EVERY ONE OF THOSE DECISIONS IS THE RIGHT ONE."

– Jeff Lawson, CEO and Co-founder of Twilio[26]

Examples of how culture influences day to day actions are everywhere:

» In a culture of respect and consideration, people make it their priority to address personal frustration constructively. Even if it's more difficult, they do it in a private face-to-face meeting, instead of in an impersonal email or in front of others.
» In a risk-averse culture, people will be slow to act, as they focus on evaluating the stakes to avoid risks.
» In a go-getting, straightforward culture, such as SWG's, we are direct and to the point in every conversation. We respect each other's time and each other and see no need to sugarcoat what we say.

Why a strong company culture matters

We often ask startup founders what benefits they associate with a strong company culture. Typically, they believe the main benefit is in recruitment: talent acquisition, retention and employer branding. After all, if you want to learn about a company's culture, you most likely find

---

26 Source: Wired. How Do You Define Startup Culture?, n.d. Retrieved from: https://www.wired.com/insights/2013/09/how-do-you-define-startup-culture/

the details on the careers page. An attractive culture may be a magnet for recruitment and culture-fit can be a good tool to use when screening candidates, but a great company culture also brings many other proven business advantages.

Making culture a key part of recruitment: Nordigen

Nordigen's co-founders **Rolands Mesters** and **Roberts Bernans** are in their early 30s. They are easy-going and very humble about becoming one of NewEurope's most promising fintech startups. They have also succeeded in developing a strong culture in their company.

Since Nordigen's culture is very important to the founders, they took pride in being involved in recruitment, devoting a significant amount of time to the process. As the company grew, demand on their time increased. They started to struggle to devote the time the recruitment process required. Two years ago, they changed the process.

While one of them still interviews the candidates, the focus of the founders' direct engagement is on role requirements. They have delegated the culture-fit interviews to the team: Up to three employees carry these out. To support the employees, Rolands and Roberts developed a range of guiding questions. However, the employees are free to drive the interviews as they please. If any of them believes there is no culture alignment, the candidate is turned down. This process not only ensures that new hires are aligned with Nordigen's culture, but reinforces company culture every time an employee carries out a culture-fit interview. Employees have become ambassadors that uphold Nordigen's company culture.

Founders often don't invest time to shape their startup culture because they overlook the fact that the benefits go far beyond recruitment. They recognise, however, that a powerful brand is a valuable business asset. Here lies the catch, which many startup founders fail to grasp: You can't deliver your brand promise without a strong, corresponding internal culture. Culture and brand are two sides of the same coin, invisibly divided only by the line between the inside and the outside of a company. The brand promise is delivered and made real by the people working in the company. If the two don't align, your promise is empty.

BRAND

is a promise to a customer.

CULTURE

is how you deliver it.

The benefits of defining these fundamental concepts to shape your culture

Defining purpose, vision and values to build a strong culture that delivers a powerful brand has additional benefits for a startup. Having these in place will:

1. Align the organisation so it can focus on its core goals

A strong culture helps co-founders and employees align on what to do and how to take those actions. It eliminates the discussions and internal politics that come with misalignment. A strong culture, therefore, helps reduce the noise and keep the focus on goals. From the time you define your values and get aligned, you can focus on your goals.

2. Provide the clarity you need to make decisions faster

In a startup, dozens of decisions are made every day. When your values are clear, the decision-making process is much more straightforward. You avoid spending time debating what to do, because your values guide you. At SWG, we look to our values every time we need to consider our options. Often this helps us make decisions easier and faster.

3. Inspire stakeholders (employees, clients, investors, partners)

When we advise startups on how to pitch, we always recommend that they start with the **Why** - their purpose. When we pitch SWG, we always follow this rule, starting with the purpose and continuing with our vision. As the CEO of SWG, Cristobal always uses the SWG purpose: "We help founders to become entrepreneurs and build great international tech companies." The **Why** resonates with the audience on a deeper level than any **What**, no matter which stakeholder he is addressing.

Companies and founders driven by the **Why** are simply inspiring, much more so than those pointing to product features or even business results. A clear purpose inspires your team, your customers, your investors and any other stakeholder.

Rolands Mesters, co-founder and the CEO of Nordigen[27], argues that having a team that is inspired, with employees who love coming to work, will deliver more for the company.

"I BELIEVE THAT IF THE TEAM LOVES WHAT THEY DO, WE WILL ACHIEVE BETTER RESULTS THAN IF WE HAD "AN ARMY" PUSHING ON THE GROWTH AND PROFITS."

- Rolands Mesters, co-founder and CEO of Nordigen

27   Nordigen is one of the most promising fintech companies in the NewEurope region. Founded in 2016, it provides services for banks and other financial institutions that enable Open Banking. Nordigen operates across 17 countries, working with 80+ global financial institutions. It has a team of 30 people, speaking eight languages. Several of them, from Spain, Portugal and Ireland, have moved to Riga to work at Nordigen.

4. Differentiate the company in the marketplace

It takes years for startups to build successful brands, if they ever succeed. Many of today's startups are very generic, from brand to product. You become genuinely differentiated in a competitive marketplace by having a unique culture and brand. The more unique, the better. Don't be afraid of sticking out. Your brand may be rejected by some potential customers, but by clearly stating where you stand, your target audience will feel a much stronger connection to your company. "We thought that if we got the culture right, then building our brand to be about the very best customer service would happen naturally on its own[28]," [which it did] Tony Hsieh, co-founder and CEO at Zappos.com[29]

5. Invigorate the organisation when times get tough

We don't know a single successful startup that has not gone through several tough periods. Many startups face near-bankruptcy and have to make difficult decisions. We know from personal experience that in these situations, it's your culture that will keep you, your team and the company going.

Imagine informing employees that the company may not be able to pay salaries for the next two months, or having to fire half of the team because there is no money. In a company with a weak culture, people will look for work elsewhere. They come to work to get a salary. When that's at risk, they leave. In a company with a strong culture, the employees will instead think about how they can get through the critical period together with you. This is a real scenario which Cristobal has been through many times. It can either be devastating or the most powerful moment of your startup CEO career.

If you leave your culture to develop on its own, there's no quick fix when 's**t hits the fan'. You can't suddenly start referring to company values if that you didn't prioritise before the crisis. By living your values daily, you will inspire the team to follow your example. Moreover, your culture will be ready for the tough times which will inevitably come.

---

28   Source: Hsieh, T., Delivering Happiness, A Path to Profits, Passion and Purpose, 2010, Grand Central Publishing.
29   Zappos.com was one of the first internet unicorns. The company started selling shoes online in 1999 and was acquired by Amazon in 2010. It just celebrated its 20 year anniversary. Tony Hsieh remains its inspiring CEO.

Choose co-founders whose values and purpose align with yours

We have looked at many great startups from NewEurope, such as TransferWise or Bolt. They are all very different from each other, but we also see similarities among founders and employees: The energy they display, the way they talk about their vision and mission, the similar attitudes and taste in music, sometimes even the way they're dressed. These trends didn't emerge on their own. In some startups, cultural attributes are left to chance, but in these successful startups, they were achieved through conscious decisions and processes.

Many co-founders ignore the need to align on the culture and values they want for their company. Often the search for a co-founder is focused on finding complementary professional skills. We notice this happening a lot, in particular with founders from NewEurope. It usually happens when individuals lack understanding of how to build a thriving, entrepreneurial company culture. Thinking only about skills is not enough.

Anna Andersone, serial entrepreneur and founder at **be-with,** a clothing line promoting hugs and physical contact and Chief Empowerment Officer at Riga TechGirls, experienced first hand the problems that can come from founders not aligning values between them. "I remember [at] my first true tech startup, we never discussed values," she says. "When things were running smoothly everything was OK. But the moment things got tough, our values were not aligned and things went astray."

A founding team is the only thing that you can't change in a business. A dysfunctional founding team in a great market means inevitable failure. Therefore, it's critical for prospective founders to spend time together to be as certain as they can be about each other before committing to working together. I have learned both from my own startup experience and by observing hundreds of teams how critical it is to have:

» a common view of purpose, vision and values as well as passion for solving the problem the startup is aiming to address.
» an understanding of each other's personal **Why** and shared values that will guide the company.
» Open-mindedness and diversity. While there is a need for commonality in the areas above, co-founders should be diverse. Avoid the human tendency to gravitate towards people who are similar to you. Look for characteristics and skill sets that are different from and complement your own.

As founders, take your time to get this right. Don't rush to find your co-founders. According to a study[30] by U.S. venture capital firm Blossom Street Ventures, it took 19 SaaS companies that went public in 2018-19 on average 11 years to exit. That means that you have, on average, more than nine years together with your co-founders if you build a successful business.

The importance of co-founder alignment: TransferGo

TransferGo is co-founder and CEO **Daumantas Dvilinskas**' 3rd venture. His previous startups had mixed results: one was partly successful, another failed. The TransferGo founders couldn't be more different in terms of character, temperament, and occasionally, points of view. There have been bumps along the way, but from day one, they always trusted one another and believed in the company's vision. "We wanted to change how people move money internationally. We all thought that if we succeed our win [would have] the potential to change people's lives", explains Daumantas.

---

30   The full study looked at equity raised by 99 SaaS companies to have gone public since 2000. Of these, 19 went public in 2018-19. Source: Blossom Street Ventures. Metrics from 99 SaaS exits, distilled, 2020. Retrieved from: https://blossomstreetventures.com/2020/05/27/metrics-from-99-saas-exits-distilled/

The TransferGo founders worked hard to put the company's interests before their personal concerns. Daumantas emphasizes that his co-founders don't have strong egos (but that we shouldn't count him in that category!), while being talented and hard working. The fact that the co-founders are aligned on the fundamentals while each contributes diverse skill sets, personalities and viewpoints have been essential to enable TransferGo to deliver in the face of constant adversity. Now the team's challenge is to build a lasting global organization, with thousands of employees. Amid all the changes TransferGo has been through, their purpose has never changed and neither has the amazing level of trust the founders have between them.

When co-founders are part of the same family, there is already a strong bond. Trust is there already - you don't need to invest time and energy building it. However, for many investors, family founders are a red flag and can even be a reason not to invest. At SWG we have had amazing experiences, as well as some negative ones, with teams involving husband and wife, siblings or father and son. Nevertheless, we are often asked whether we invest if a startup's co-founders are related.

One of the fastest-growing startups in the SWG portfolio, ZITICITY[31], is a case in point. ZITICITY is a B2B[32] supply chain startup, originally from Lithuania. It developed a presence in four countries in less than 15 months and, at the time of writing, it is in the process of raising Series A funding. The company has three co-founders: Brothers **Laimonas and Vytautas Noreika**, CEO and COO respectively, and CTO **Karolis Januskas.**

From the beginning, Laimonas recognised that to create a winning team, it was imperative to understand the underlying values and motivation of each co-founder. For him, bringing on board a family member was a win-win situation. "Building a company with someone you played, fought, dreamt and learned together [with] for the past 31 years makes things a lot easier," explains Laimonas. "You can trust each

---

31   ZITICITY delivers items to your customers in less than 1 hour using crowd-source delivery fleets in every major European city.
32   Business to Business.

other 100%. Brothers are not afraid to challenge each other internally, while externally being a rock-solid team ready for any situation."

While we understood the advantages of having your sibling as your co-founder, we wondered how easy it was to bring in the third co-founder, Karolis, and to make him feel equal. Laimonas emphasizes the importance of having up-front conversations to make sure that all co-founders are aligned on aims and values. In their case, they had the same level of ambition and desire to create impact while having some fun in the process. It was less about short term financial comfort and more about building a global tech success story to inspire the next generation of founders.

In the end, Karolis was the first of the three co-founders to leave his well-paid corporate job and start coding for ZITICITY full-time. Laimonas stresses how important it was for the three founders to live and work together in the early days to cement their bond. For them, the opportunity to move to Tallinn for four months during their time with SWG fast-tracked not only the ZITICITY business. It strengthened their personal relationship.

Set the fundamentals for a strong culture immediately

Once you form a company, a discussion around purpose, vision, values needs to be on the agenda from the get-go. Yet, many founders, especially first-time founders, think that all focus should be put on product development and finding product-market fit[33]. Unconsciously, they are making a tradeoff. They try to skip culture, as it's developing anyway. They believe it's something they can focus on down the road – perhaps when they hit 50 or 100 employees.

---

[33] Product-market fit is the degree to which a product satisfies a strong market demand.

If you want your startup to be successful, start building your company culture as early as possible. Researchers from Velocity[34] used data from the Traversing the Traction Gap Institute (TGI[35]), in a 2018 study to show that **among successful startups in Silicon Valley, 82% started building their culture on day one.**

Brian Cesky, CEO and co-founder of the global room-rental phenomenon AirBnB, addressed this in a 2014 lecture at Stanford[36]. An early focus on culture was part of his company's success. That included interviewing all potential employees to make sure they were fitting the culture: "We finished Y Combinator in April 2009 [and] hired our first engineer in July...Some people ask why did you spend so much time on hiring your first engineer. I think bringing in your first engineer is like bringing in a DNA chip to the company."

Build your culture to attract the right people: Miro

Miro is an online collaborative whiteboard platform that enables distributed teams to work together effectively. Miro has a team of nearly 300 people and has raised over US$75 million in funding so far. It has become extremely popular during the Coronavirus pandemic[37].

Andrey Khusid, Miro Founder & CEO, stresses that culture needs to be built early. "Day one is the right time to start deciding on values and crafting the culture you want your startup to have," he says. "A company's culture and values help it attract the right people for its mission, and since the earliest team members pass the cultural torch down to later hires, you need to build your cultural foundation early." In Miro's case, Andrey had his vision clear from the start: "I wanted...a product-led company with a customer-centric approach to

---

34 A research and consulting firm based in Silicon Valley.
35 Traversing the Traction Gap, Bruce Cleveland and Wildcat Venture Partners.
36 Brian Chesky, Founder of Airbnb, and Alfred Lin, Former COO of Zappos and Partner at Sequoia Capital discussed how to build a great company culture at Stanford University Lecture. The recording available at: https://www.youtube.com/watch?time_continue=1000&v=RfWgVWGEuGE&feature=emb_logo and the transcript at: https://genius.com/
37 Source: MENAFN.Must have Remote Working Tools, 2020. Retrieved from: https://menafn.com/1100214110/Must-have-Remote-Working-Tools

innovation and strong collaboration, and as a result, people with similar values are the ones who are drawn to Miro and who ultimately stay and thrive here."

While the ideal is to start defining your culture as soon as a startup is formed, now is always better than never. Sellfy, a B2B company providing quick, hassle free online stores, found that its lack of defined purpose, vision and values became a problem when it started to grow rapidly. Founded in 2012, it had annual recurrent revenues of more than €1 million in 2020. At the time of writing, it is seeing 10-20% quarterly revenue growth. Recognising the need to set clear foundations for Sellfy's culture, CEO **Maris Dagis** turned to Cristobal, who sits on the Sellfy board, for advice. Using the PERFORM methodology to help define these concepts made a huge difference, explains Maris: "Once we worked on our culture, it brought us much closer together as a team, aligned our efforts and created a strong drive to achieve more," he says. "I would love to go back and work on culture much earlier in our journey, but it is never too late to do so, and I believe it will always bring you value to work on culture no matter when."

At SWG, Purpose and Vision were defined early on, but we took longer to get to our values. Both externally and internally, there was a sense that we had a strong culture but we couldn't describe it. While we were growing, we also learned the hard way that defined values were needed: some people left who had excellent skills but didn't connect with our culture. We couldn't explain why.

We had to make sure we could all describe our values and culture in a similar way. In the middle of 2017, the SWG team consisted of 12 people. Cristobal knew we couldn't wait any longer to make sure that new people joining our team were aligned with our values. We took the team to an offsite in Spain and got to work.

"DAY ONE IS THE RIGHT
TIME TO START DECIDING
ON VALUES AND CRAFTING
THE CULTURE YOU WANT
YOUR STARTUP TO HAVE"

- Andrey Khusid, Founder & CEO of Miro

Practical exercises to help set a strong foundation for your startup

This series of exercises will help your company start the discussion to define purpose, vision and values. At SWG, we do these exercises together with our startup teams after running the content of this chapter as a workshop. We like dedicating a couple of hours to this and have at least all co-founders together to start the discussion.

However, this is just a starting point. It will spark discussion and create an appetite for more. Ideally, take your co-founders and all your employees for an offsite to work through it. The more you involve your entire team in this discussion, the more impactful the results will be. Your team will feel committed to the journey ahead.

The value of offsites for culture: Ondato

Liudas Kanapienis, CEO and co-founder Ondato[38], a recently named 'Fintech leader of the year' at the Lithuanian 2020 Fintech Awards, notes that it's easy to think that it isn't important to have a full-team offsite session dedicated to culture.

"But when you have it, you ask yourself 'why we did not make it happen before'," he says. "Even though you think you share the vision and mission every day with your team, it is only when you stand back a bit from your daily operations that you have the

---

[38]   Ondato is a promising fintech startup in NewEurope, becoming leader in a new category: Fintech Compliance CRM. The company's revenues have grown 300% over the past 12 months.

right set up. Then you can actually talk about such important things as vision, mission, internal culture, external culture, targets - where and how we are moving forward, engaging the entire team. This was impossible to achieve by just simply talking everyday during the operations or daily standup."
Using the PERFORM Methodology made the offsite productive. "Leveraging the PERFORM exercises for these workshops was instrumental in making the most out of this meaningful time", he adds.

Defining your purpose - The Why

These are a few suggested exercises to help define your WHY. It can be challenging to have a conversation about purpose. When delivering the Purpose and Values Workshop to SWG startups, we always start with a few warm-up exercises to gently introduce some of the concepts and get into the right frame of mind.

Exercise 1: Warm-up: Your personal WHY

In this exercise, each person reflects over why they joined the company.

Step 1: Each person reflects individually and writes down their personal reasons.

Step 2: Share and discuss as a group.

Exercise 2: Warm-up: Your startup as an animal

Ask yourself: If your company was an animal, what animal would it be?

Step 1: Each person imagines an animal. It can be real or fictional: Unleash the imagination! Individually, each person writes down which animal they've chosen, as well as the reason they chose it. What positive and negative characteristics does it have that you find in the company?

Step 2: Share and discuss as a group.

Step 3: As a group, agree which animal to use to represent your startup.

CyberStruggle's choice: The Honeybadger

In its your startup as an animal exercise, CyberStruggle, a Turkish cybersecurity startup developing onsite and online training courses for Cybersecurity professionals based on Navy Seals-type training, chose the Honeybadger as the animal to represent it. CEO and co-founder **Kubilay Onur Gungor** explains: "The honey badger is notorious for its strength, ferocity and toughness. When escape is impossible it is known for its vicious and fearless attacks, allegedly even repelling much larger predators such as lions and hyenas."

Cyberstruggle has an eagle on its logo, but the Honeybadger resonates more strongly with Kubilay. "I feel more like the honey badger," he says. "They don't give a damn, they always fight, always find a way, never give up and have a passion for their loved ones."

Exercise 3: Purpose

Step 1: Working individually, answer the following questions:
What is the **Why** of your startup? (Your **Purpose**)
What is the impact you want to have?

Step 2: Share with your co-founders and discuss what your company really stands for.

Step 3: Define your Purpose. Keep it short, inspirational and concrete.

Setting your vision - your What

Once you have defined your company's purpose, setting the Vision will help bring clarity and make your purpose tangible. The vision should be concrete and ambitious. A compelling vision is inspiring and helps fire up your team. Based on the vision, you can set the strategic goals that keep your business on track.

Exercise 4: Your Boldest Vision

In a few words, explain what you want your startup to achieve

Step 1: Write down individually where do you see your startup 3, 5 or 10 years from now, if everything goes to plan.

Step 2: Share with your co-founders and discuss.

Step 3: Define a short, inspirational and concrete vision.

Agreeing Purpose & Vision between family founders: Simporter

Simporter, a startup providing data analytics for FMCG (fast-moving consumer goods) companies was set up by father-and-son team **Tim and Dillon Hall.** They spent a lot of time talking through each step of the Purpose and Values exercises to ensure they were aligned.

"At the very beginning, we spent long hours talking about our company's purpose and vision," Tim and Dillon explained in an email. "We did not rush over this to start with execution. The first thing was to make sure we had the same timeline in mind. It's not uncommon for a company where the father wants a lifestyle income-producing business, and the son wants a growth company. Here we were on the same page: we both wanted a venture-backed rapid growth company with an exit in about 5 years."

The next step they took was to consider impact. "Not in terms of a lofty social goal – world peace or reversing climate change," they clarify, "but not in purely commercial terms either. The impact we wanted to make was to replace inefficient human tasks for product management with really useful data." Tim and Dillon wanted to make life easier for product teams by streamlining the way the teams work. "So they can focus on the creative stuff and leave the analysis to our machine learning model," they state. "We envisioned a future where everybody in [Consumer Packaged Goods]/FMCG relies on our dashboard for forecasting and concept development the way brokers and traders rely on Bloomberg terminals."

Fast forward two years and Simporter is growing by nearly 20-30% quarterly and generating €70,000 in monthly recurring revenue. It employs 20 people in three different countries. The founders are in discussions about a series A funding round and we're confident their annual recurring revenue will be €5 million within the next 2-3 years.

Defining values: The How, or your company's fundamental beliefs

Defining values is often a process rather than something that is covered in a one-off session, but this exercise will help set you on the right path. You can also add to it by addressing your not Values: what will you not tolerate and what do you not want to be associated with?

Exercise 5: Values

This exercise is focused on choosing words that describe your company. It should cover both how your company is now and what it aspires to be like.

Step 1: Write down individually the top 5 values of your startup.

Step 2: Discuss them with your team and align on 3 to 5 values.

Step 3: Phrase them so that the language mean something to you.

Step 4: Do the first 3 steps again for the Values you will **never** tolerate.

Doing a version of this exercise at SWG, we divided our teams into three groups, depending on how long they had been with the company. Each group spent two hours on the exercise before we got together and shared the results. The initial outcome was nine values.

This was too many. Instead, over time we divided them into two sets:

» Four organizational values or what we believe in
» Five operational values, or "This is how we act".

This is by no means a recommendation or a best practice, but it works for us at SWG.

Living your culture daily and embedding it across your team

Defining and formalizing your purpose, vision and values to build a strong culture is just the beginning of the journey. As a CEO or co-founder, you need to live it every day. You also need to reinforce the culture in your company, so that every team member lives it, too.

The more time you spend on culture upfront, the less time you'll spend trying to fix it in the long term. Building a great culture is like flossing your teeth: a few minutes of attention each day will save you from painful, costly, and time-consuming crises down the line.

As your culture matures, you'll start to notice culture-related rituals emerging that have nothing to do with the founders. Encourage this: it means your culture is thriving. Empower your team to celebrate your company's values in its own way.

Remember that every day, you are a walking example for your company culture and values. This is especially important during tough times. Performance discussions with your team members should focus as much on whether they live the values as to whether they perform well in their job.

At the time of writing, we are in the middle of the Covid-19 crisis. A crisis like this demands strong leadership. Use values as part of your narrative, live them fully and show that they are more important than ever.

KEY TAKEAWAYS

» When a company has a strong **Why (Purpose),** a clear and compelling **What (Vision)** and it operates with a set of values and a clear **How (Values),** it will develop a powerful working culture.

» To ensure **that founders are aligned and develop trust** between them, culture and values discussions need to be **part of the company's agenda from the start.** The more time you spend on values and culture upfront, the less time you'll spend trying to fix it in the long term.

» Make sure you have a **founding team with complementary skill sets and characters.** The founding team needs to have a shared vision for the business and a passion for solving the client's pain. Beyond that, diversity is key.

» **You can't deliver a brand promise if you don't have a strong internal culture.** Culture and brand are inseparable,

» Having a **strong culture** that delivers a strong brand **has 5 clear, tangible benefits. It:**
1. Helps to align an organisation so it can focus on its goals;
2. Provides a clear roadmap which gives you decision making shortcuts;
3. Inspires stakeholders (employees, clients, investors, partners);
4. Differentiates the company in the marketplace;
5. Invigorates the organisation when times get tough.

» **Start the journey by defining a clear purpose and an ambitious vision.** This brings clarity and direction. Make sure the founders also agree on the timeline.

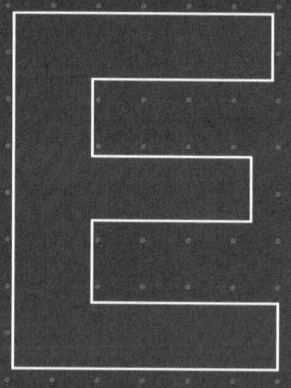

EFFECTIVE PLANNING

IN THIS CHAPTER, YOU WILL LEARN:

» Why it is important to plan consistently as a startup founder
» What mindset you should develop in to be an effective planner
» Why the most successful founders set ambitious goals
» Long term planning strategies and examples
» How to organize your day with the **PERFORM** planning method (PPM)

"PLANNING IS BRINGING THE FUTURE INTO THE PRESENT SO THAT YOU CAN DO SOMETHING ABOUT IT NOW.[39]"

*- **Alan Lakein**, author, How to Get Control of Your Time and Your Life*

---

39   Lakein, A. Alan Lakein Quotes. BrainyQuote.com, 2020. Retrieved from: https://www.brainyquote.com/quotes/alan_lakein_154655

The importance of targets and planning

Effective Planning
The process of deciding in advance what's most important to be done and how to achieve it by spending minimal effort and resources.

"All this planning is great, but I don't have time to plan my time. We are just so busy".
-A typical excuse from an overwhelmed startup founder

Does the quote sound familiar? We've worked with hundreds of startup teams. Most founders don't enjoy spending time planning, especially in early stages. It's a lot more fun to work on building the product and execute on the ideas you're passionate about. You show up at the office and immediately start **doing** things, often without having a clear direction.

Remember the jungle metaphor from the first chapter? When you start your own company, you go into the startup jungle. Your task is to survive, but you aspire to build something meaningful in the long run.
You are right to work hard and make progress every day. But to succeed and reach your long term goal, you also need to stop, get a sense of perspective and figure out how to maximize your limited resources. That's where planning comes into play.
You might have seen one of those movies in which adventurers are hustling through the jungle. At one point they stop, climb a tree and try to see the full picture of what they're facing. It might take them 15 or 30 minutes, but it's time worth spending, because it helps them evaluate the situation and focus on what matters. In your startup, you'll have to invest time in planning every quarter, every week and every day. This time investment will always pay dividends.

Without clear goals and a plan for how to achieve them, you risk wasting time working on tasks which aren't important. You end up being busy, but not productive. Constant goal setting and planning is vital to make sure you use your limited resources effectively.

This chapter will explore practical planning mindsets, methods and techniques that will help you stay on top of your priorities and allocate resources accordingly. The level of detail in your planning might differ depending on company stage, team size and priorities.

The mindset of an effective planner

To become a planning wizard, you need to adopt the right mindset. Focusing on the outcome and being ready to adapt to any changes will put you on track.

Taking an outcome-driven approach

"ONE OF THE THINGS WE UNDERSTOOD AS A STARTUP IS THAT IF YOU DON'T HAVE A CLEAR VISION AND OBJECTIVES, IT IS VERY EASY TO GET CAUGHT UP DOING LOW PRIORITY TASKS."

- Artis Kehris, co-founder & COO of Printify[40]

---

40   Printify is a Latvian technology platform that simplifies and automates print-on-demand services for online merchants.

You can't deliver results effectively if you are not clear about what you are trying to achieve. You can only get the clarity you need if you allocate the time needed to plan and achieve it.

Going back to the jungle: imagine you have a bow, but only a few arrows. In order to eat, you need to hunt. Rather than aim for larger game, you shoot at anything that moves and end up with an inedible, scrawny bird. You've worked hard, but there's nothing to show for it. This of course seems like a foolish thing to do, but it is very similar to the risk you'd be taking as a founder if you're working hard with no clear aim.

As a founder, it's your job to **always start with the end in mind** - be clear about the **outcome** you are working towards. One of the definitions of 'outcome'[41] is 'The final product or end result'. Any action you take, or don't take, will have a consequence or an outcome. If you don't intentionally strive towards a specific outcome, that outcome might not be what's needed. Without a goal, you can waste a lot of your limited resources on doing what that shouldn't be done at all. Without a plan for how to reach your goal, you're likely to be less efficient. Aiming for specific outcomes and planning how to get there gives your startup a much greater chance of success.

The foundation of productivity: David Allen

At a speaker's dinner at a conference in Graz, Austria, Stoyan had the chance to chat with **David Allen**, productivity guru and creator of the Getting Things Done[42] (GTD) methodology. Allen stressed: "**Outcomes** and **actions** are the zeros and ones and the ultimate reduction of productivity. What are we trying to produce as an experience or as a result? And what do we need to do now to allocate our resources, our intention, our focus, our activity to make sure that happens."

41   The definition retrieved from Dictionary.com:
https://www.dictionary.com/browse/outcome
42   Getting Things Done is a famous productivity methodology.

Adaptability and navigating change

The startup environment is very dynamic and fast moving. Your plans today might not be viable tomorrow. To get into the right mindset you need to have clear goals, but stay flexible, nimble and ready to change them if the context changes. Many of us had set goals for 2020. Then Covid-19 hit, creating an unprecedented global pandemic. We all had to adapt to the new environment.

You can't stick to the same plan when circumstances change. As legendary 19th century Prussian military commander **Helmuth von Moltke** stated[43]: "No plan survives contact with the enemy." He asserted that commanders could only plan the beginning of a campaign in detail. From there, it's the role of the leader to adjust rapidly as reality unfolds. Nevertheless, it remains important to have a plan in the first place.

"A BAD PLAN IS STILL ALWAYS BETTER THAN NO PLAN AT ALL. HAVE A PLAN. YOU CAN ALWAYS CHANGE IT. BUT DON'T JUST PRETEND THAT EVERYTHING ABOUT THE FUTURE IS RANDOM. IF YOU SAY THAT EVERYTHING IS RANDOM AND OUT OF YOUR CONTROL, THAT'S A WAY YOU SET

---

43   Source: Moltke, H. On Strategy (1870), part of Militarische Werke - Military Works, 1900.

YOURSELF UP FOR FAILURE."

- **Peter Theil**, *billionaire Investor and co-founder of* **Paypal**.[44]

Set ambitious goals and clarify your priorities

The power of aiming high

"Shoot for the moon. Even if you miss it, you will end up among the stars[45]",
- **Norman Vincent Peale**, American Author and Minister

As someone who grew up in the post-communist Balkans, Stoyan was never encouraged to dream big and set audacious goals. Instead, the culture encouraged a mindset of humility. You should set reasonable goals and make sure you hit them. The assumption was that if you're aiming too high and fail, you'll be considered a fraud or a failure.
When we run PERFORM workshops with startups from NewEurope, the section on ambitious goals is usually one of the highest rated. It helps the founders expand their horizons, understand what's possible and get reassurance that they're not the only ones with high ambitions.

The fact is that no one achieved anything of great significance by being reasonable and aiming low. Think about any great founder. One of the reasons they succeeded was their ability to envision a more expansive, innovative future. They imagined entirely new, game-changing

44 Source: Theil, P. Interview given for Forbes. Available at:
https://youtu.be/JqxzLUE6pP8
45 Source: Peale, N.V. Norman Vincent Peale Quotes. Goodreads, n.d. Retrieved from:https://www.goodreads.com/quotes/4324-shoot-for-the-moon-even-if-you-miss-you-ll-land

solutions that they broke down into goals the team could focus its execution on, no matter how unreasonable the end-result might have seemed.

Having unreasonable goals doesn't make you crazy.

In 2003, it was unreasonable to think you could have a conference call with another human through an internet platform. Fortunately the **Skype** founders **Niklas Zennström and Janus Friis** saw things differently and today videoconferencing is a normal part of our daily life.

In 2013, It was audacious for a 19-year old from a small Baltic state to think they could build a competing global empire from Europe just as Uber was starting to expand globally. Fortunately **Markus Villig**, at the time a 19 year-old Estonian student, had an ambitious vision and at the time of writing, **Bolt** (previously Taxify) has more than 1,500 employees and a valuation of €1.9 billion.

It used to be unreasonable to think you could make millions by detecting and correcting grammar, spelling and punctuation errors. Fortunately, Ukranian founders **Alex Shevchenko, Max Lytvyn, and Dmytro Lider** didn't listen to the naysayers. Today, in 2020, **Grammarly** has almost 7 million daily active users and is valued at over €1 billion.

But let's not be blinded by these examples: Even if you put in years of hard work and have the support of a team with world-class talent, it's rare to achieve this level of success. However, it's more than possible to build a great international company. To do so, you need to stop trying to be reasonable and start being ambitious instead. Ambitious targets are in fact practical.
Setting an ambitious vision and corresponding goals can help you and your team focus on the activities that really matter and achieve better results. Even if you don't end up getting all the way to an ambitious target, you have a much greater chance to end up closer to it than you would with a pragmatic goal.
Imagine that you are currently making €8,000 in monthly recurring revenue (MRR) and your aim is to reach €10,000 MRR in six months. What if you decided your goal was to reach €50,000 in six months

instead. How would you act differently? What would you change in the way you are working?

The advantage of reaching for the stars: Printify

Printify is a Latvian dropshipping and printing service for e-commerce. The company's co-founder and COO, **Artis Kehris**, explains that Printify has been lucky to have a number of experienced Silicon Valley veterans as investors, such as **Gokul Rajaram**, known as the "Godfather of Adsense" and **Steve Chen**, co-founder of Youtube. These investors pushed the Printify founders to raise their standards and expand their vision. According to Artis, the way they challenged the team to think bigger helped Printify accelerate its growth.

When the company generated revenues of around €10 million in 2018, Gokul asked them to present a roadmap showing how the team would grow the figure to €50 million, €100 million and €500 million. "Just by thinking of how to achieve these larger goals, you start coming up with bigger ideas. You can't sweat the small stuff anymore. You don't have time for that," Artis says. "It gave us a mindset, so we were thinking: We are at €10 million now. We can definitely do €100 million. We have a pretty good understanding of how to get to €500 million. We have a vision of how to get to €1 billion and we are actually convinced that we can do it. When you have that mindset, it's so much easier to decide what's important to do this year, next year and what main pillars we should focus on. "

Using audacious goals to maximize results is not a new concept. A great example is the story of the Japanese Bullet train: Shinkansen. At the beginning of the 1960s, inspired to make the nation one of the world's innovation leaders, the Japanese government set the country's best engineers an unreasonable goal: build a train that can accelerate to 200 km per hour and have it ready to transport passengers by the time of the Olympic Games in Tokyo in 1964. At the time, the fastest train in the world could do 110 km per hour.

With this audacious goal and a strict deadline, the engineers started on the project. They had no choice but to find a way to make it work. After a few years of hard work and commitment, applying hundreds of bold iterations and innovations, they finally achieved the seemingly unreasonable goal.

Nobody is inspired by a modest goal, but by setting an audacious goal, you can engage people to join and support you in making it happen.

Exercise: The 10x Your Goal

Step 1: Pick a time frame (For example the next month or quarter) and think about the most important goal you need to achieve within that time.

Step 2: Multiply the goal by 10.

Step 3: Brainstorm ideas and opportunities. What has to happen for you to achieve it?

Step 4: Have a good look at the ideas. Which ones are practical and could be implemented if they were developed further?

Clarity makes your team effective

The dynamic life of a founder exposes you to a constant stream of new information, thoughts, ideas and decisions. It's easy to forget that the rest of the team might not have attended the last meeting and might not see the big picture the same way you do. Yet we sometimes see founders act as if the team can read their minds, instead of putting together a plan and communicating it.

Andrey Sergeyev[46] is the author of Have a Meaningful Workday. In an interview for Stoyan's podcast[47] Andrey outlined an exercise he loves to do with leaders and their teams. He asks everyone to individually write down the company's top priority for that year. Most of the time, the leaders are shocked to realize that almost everyone writes down a different priority.

---

46 Andrey Sergeyev is an Entrepreneur, Digital Business Strategy & Leadership Advisor, International Speaker.
47 Stoyan is the founder and host of the podcast: 'Productivity Mastery'.

"AS A CEO IN A FAST GROWING ORGANISATION, I HAVE TO CONSTANTLY IMPROVE MY ABILITY TO DELEGATE. IT'S NOT ALWAYS EASY,
BUT IT FEELS AMAZING WHEN YOU GET THE HANG OF IT AND REALISE THAT OTHERS CAN SOLVE MANY THINGS BETTER THAN YOU."

– Mette Lykke, CEO at Too Good To Go

As a former movie producer, Stoyan knows how important it is to get everyone in the team on board with what needs to be done and how it's being done. Every professional film-maker knows that you can't go on set before you have a confirmed screenplay, storyboard, art direction, production schedule and so on. It's equally important that the plan has been well communicated to the team.

The tools provide clarity and alignment. They're essential because no matter how much we plan, anything can happen when we go on set. We might have to do extra takes. We might experience problems with the lights or the location.

Original Files from the Production of "Arene"[48]

SCREENPLAY

INT. AIRCRAFT

The aircraft cabin hold is dark and cramped. Long and narrow fixtures in the ceiling light the interior in a gloomy blue. In the back, two soldiers are seated, ISAAC "ISKY" FAY (25) and DAVID CHEUNG (27) and leaning against a wall in front of them, (COL) JAMES GIBSON (45). Seated on the floor, facing towards the soldiers, a young woman, ARENE (19), her skin and clothes dirty and her hands cuffed.

                    GIBSON
          (Into headset)
          One captive. Female. Early
          20s. Looks like one of the
          tribals. Sending you her stats
          right now.

                                        /CUT TO

CU of ARENE's face. Eyes downcast.

EXT. OVER ABANDONED CITY

The aircraft flies under a huge suspension bridge. An array of vehicles is scattered over it. Nothing moves.

INT. AIRCRAFT
                    GIBSON
          (Into headset - hesitant)
          I understand.

STORYBOARD

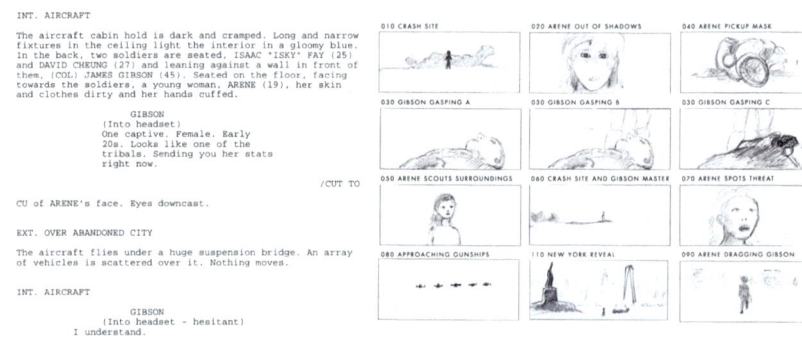

ART DIRECTION

PRODUCTION PLAN

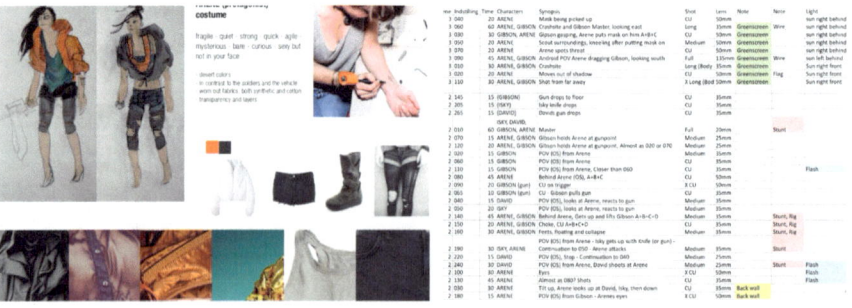

48   Arene is a Sci-Fi short film, directed by Henrik Bjerregaard Clausen with art director Lyuba Halacheva. The film is a production of 3D College Denmark, produced by Stoyan Yankov in 2015.

Stoyan once had to shoot a fantasy commercial for a Danish company. The crew was in the middle of a forest and had everything set up when the smoke machine[49] broke. They lost two hours of a very tight schedule waiting for a replacement. Choices had to be made, but this was much easier when everyone knew which scenes were the core priorities and which angles were 'nice to haves'. Despite the unexpected delays, the team got all the shots it needed to create a great final video. Entrepreneurship is similar to movie production. To be a pro, you have to be an effective planner, every week, every day and every hour.

When priorities are clearly set and the team is aligned with them, there's no need for micromanagement. To improve your delegation skills, you need to learn to let go of the urge to control everything. You hired the people on your team. Give them the opportunity to show up and do their job. When you're clear over the desired outcome and the delivery deadline, you can delegate. It's worth considering what system you want to put in place to make sure everyone in your organisation pulls in the same direction. We have shared below how Talentuno does it, but every company is different and you need to find your own system to ensure clarity and alignment.
Next, we'll look at how to do this in practice, by defining your long-term goals and breaking them down into daily tasks.

Setting the priorities right: Talentuno

Zsolt Kelliar is the founder & CEO of Talentuno, a Hungarian talent platform using crowdsourcing to find talent. He has made it his mission to ensure that priorities are clear for everyone in his team. "One of the most important lessons I learned from my mentor and investor Joe Wilson [a former Microsoft executive] is that my job as a CEO is to make sure we set the priorities right," he says. "All the guys in my C-level team know what their focus [areas] should be and how much energy and resources they should allocate to each one."

---

49   The scenes Stoyan's team was shooting required the usage of a smoke machine to create a "magical environment". You can find the video "The End was The Beginning" on Youtube:
https://youtu.be/gd3d2sNW5nw

Talentuno's C-level team meets every month. Each executive pitches up to five suggested team priorities for the month. Everyone asks questions and gives feedback before they align on each team's priorities. A file with the management team's decisions is then made available to everyone in the company. Talentuno stipulates that every team should spend 90% of its time making progress on its core priorities.

Example of monthly priorities in Talentuno

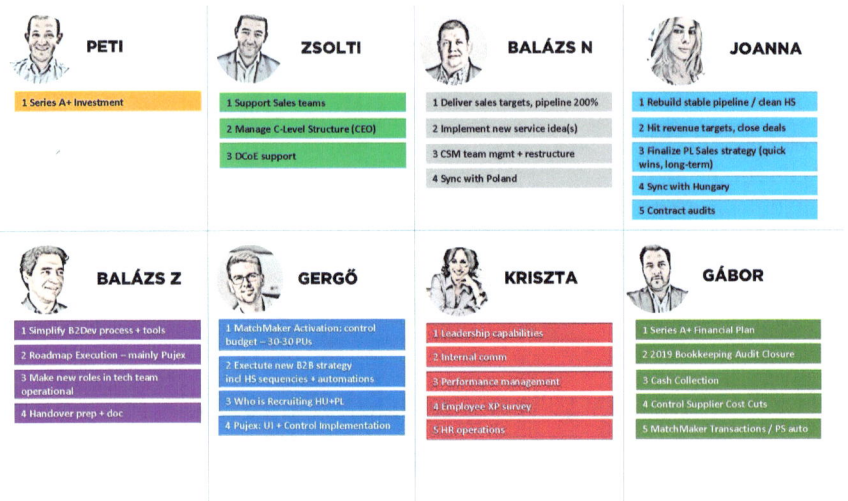

PETI

1 Series A+ Investment

ZSOLTI

1 Support Sales teams
2 Manage C-Level Structure (CEO)
3 DCoE support

BALÁZS N

1 Deliver sales targets, pipeline 200%
2 Implement new service idea(s)
3 CSM team mgmt + restructure
4 Sync with Poland

JOANNA

1 Rebuild stable pipeline / clean HS
2 Hit revenue targets, close deals
3 Finalize PL Sales strategy (quick wins, long-term)
4 Sync with Hungary
5 Contract audits

BALÁZS Z

1 Simplify B2Dev process + tools
2 Roadmap Execution – mainly Pujex
3 Make new roles in tech team operational
4 Handover prep + doc

GERGŐ

1 MatchMaker Activation: control budget – 30-30 PUs
2 Exectute new B2B strategy incl HS sequences + automations
3 Who is Recruiting HU+PL
4 Pujex: UI + Control Implementation

KRISZTA

1 Leadership capabilities
2 Internal comm
3 Performance management
4 Employee XP survey
5 HR operations

GÁBOR

1 Series A+ Financial Plan
2 2019 Bookkeeping Audit Closure
3 Cash Collection
4 Control Supplier Cost Cuts
5 MatchMaker Transactions / PS auto

„Rule of thumb" for priorization

C-Level Executives should spend approx. the below % of their time personally getting involved and driving progress in the following areas, solving challenges

Prio 1	30%
Prio 2	25%
Prio 3	15%
Prio 4	10%
Prio 5	10%
All others	10%

- **Prio 1 and Prio 2:** superfast progress expected (almost daily improvements, tracking, fast response times and resolutions)
- **Prio 3-5:** fast progress and weekly improvements expected

- It doesn't mean that only these 5 areas need to progress in their departments, but all other areas shall be delegated and receive minimum C-level personal attention

- **Recommendation:** Check your calendar in the beginning of every week, clean out the unrelated items and book dedicated time for these areas

From long-term goals to daily tasks

"Don't start your day until you have it finished...Plan your day.[50]"
- **Jim Rohn[51]**, Personal Development Guru

Planning is a constant activity

As we've outlined, successful startups spend time every day planning how to move towards their goals. To avoid getting lost in the startup jungle, get above the treeline: Set aside time to get the perspective you need to plan:

---

50   Source: Rohn, J. Jim Rohn Quotes. Az Quotes. n.d. Retrieved from: https://www.azquotes.com/quote/1460228
51   Jim Rohn (1930 - 2009) is an entrepreneur, author and motivational speaker.

- Once a day, climb a tree, looking around you to make sense of things. Measure progress, evaluate the best road ahead and set objectives for the next day.

- Once a week, climb a hill. It takes some time, but helps you see the bigger picture. You see patterns and possibilities. You have space to discuss and prioritise your next steps.

- Every quarter[52], go higher up - climb a mountain to see further. Have a strategy session. Apart from the breath-taking views and benefits for your team spirit, you have a chance to evaluate where you are. Are you moving at the right pace? What strategic direction should you take? Which opportunity will get you where you want to be?

When you plan, you build backwards. Start by envisioning the long term future and bring it back to the present. Let's look at a couple of tools that can help you.

From Long-Term Goals to Operational Planning: Too Good To Go

Mette Lykke is the CEO of Too Good to Go[53] and former co-founder and CEO of Endomondo[54]. Mette believes effective planning is a key to success for any organization.
"A major challenge I'm sure we all have is spending time on what is important and not just what is urgent and comes in from the side." Mette says. And adds:
"I address this by keeping our annual company goals constantly on top of my to-do list, as a reminder of where we're going, and breaking them down into my quarterly priorities. Then I can split the quarterly themes into a weekly to-do list. The trick here is not to be too optimistic: the list should take into account how much "crunch time" you have vs. meeting time. If a week is packed with meetings, then I'll only have evening hours to work on the list and that should be reflected in the

---

52   Keep in mind these are just example time frames. They can vary depending on the specifics of your startup.
53   Too Good To Go is a Social Impact company fighting global food waste, mostly known as the world's largest B2C marketplace for surplus food.
54   Endomondo is a fitness GPS tracking app, acquired by Under Armour for USD 80 million in 2015.

ambition level. There is no reason to demoralise yourself. Friday afternoon I clean up and make the list for the following week before the weekend. A few things may slip over to the next week and that's ok. I don't beat myself up about that."

Effective planning tools

Goal pyramids

Goal pyramids are very useful, especially for early stage founders. They provide focus and teach you to plan by **starting with the end goal**. We will look at using the pyramid to set quarterly, monthly and weekly goals.

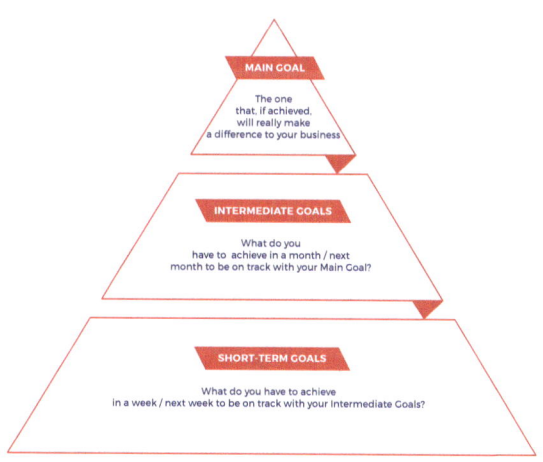

Step 1: Choose ONE goal for the next quarter

Gather your team and brainstorm potential quarterly goals. Select one as the most important goal to achieve in the next 3 months
For example: **Launch the Product**

Step 2: **Choose supporting monthly sub-goals**
Now you build backwards. Map out the sub-goals you have to achieve each month to be on track to achieve your quarterly goal.
For example:
1. Get feedback from 200 customers
2. Create a draft for the landing page
3. Hire two developers

Step 3: **Choose your weekly tasks and activities**
What do you have to achieve next week, or each week in the quarter to be on track to achieve your monthly sub-goals?
For example: for the monthly sub-goal **Get feedback from 200 customers:**
- Improve the powerpoint presentation
- Reach out to 100 customers to request feedback every week
- Get feedback from 50 customers every week
Each pyramid is focused on one main goal only. If you have more than one, create multiple pyramids. Each team in the startup can also use this tool to build a plan around their main team goals.

OKRs

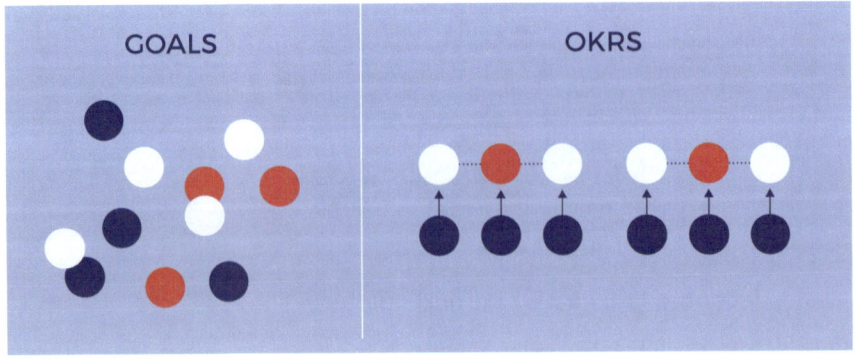

When your startup starts to grow there's usually a need for a more sophisticated method.

Many founders from NewEurope are applying the system of OKRs. OKRs[55] stands for **Objectives and Key Results**.

Objectives are usually abstract. They aim to motivate the team and provide direction.

They are short, inspirational and memorable. For example: **Unstoppable Customer Acquisition**

Key Results, on the other hand, are measurable, tangible and concise. They make the objectives specific. For example: **Attract 1,000 new customers**

Action Steps are the concrete steps you need to take to achieve your key results.

For example: **Reach out to 20,000 potential customers with a paid online marketing campaign**

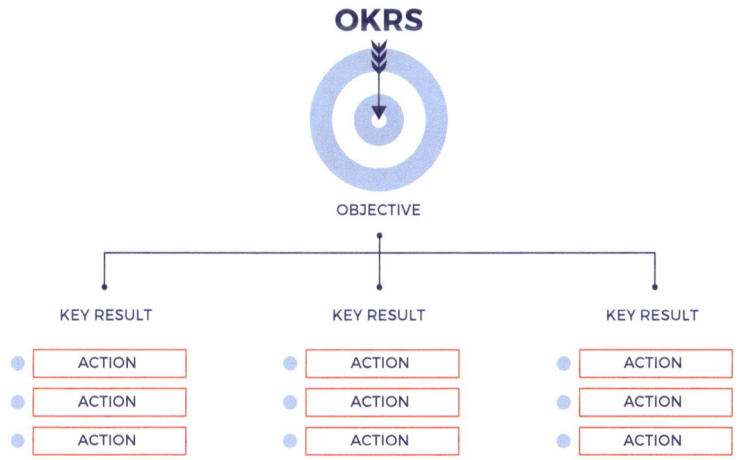

55   OKRs gained a lot of momentum in recent years, after being used successfully in Google, Intel, Spotify, LinkedIn and many other companies.

OKRs can be very useful, but with this or any other methodology: get inspired, but don't follow it blindly. Experiment and adapt it to your own context

OKRs in action: Nordigen

Roberts Bernans is co-founder and CPO of Nordigen, the data analytics startup we introduced in the previous chapter. In the very early stages, Nordigen struggled to define the company's focus and direction. Wrestling with the challenge, Roberts and the team tried different approaches before settling on a system similar to OKRs.

The company is driven by its long term vision, which they call the **North Star**. Every quarter, the senior management team meets and defines the objectives for the quarter which they label **Collective Objectives**. They communicate these objectives to the team leads. Every team is given freedom to define their own **Key Results** and **Action Steps**, which they present to the senior management team for approval. Everyone is welcome to challenge them, provide feedback and suggest ideas.

Roberts explains that this process gives each team the opportunity to see how they can support each other as they jointly work towards the Collective Objectives. The team at Nordigen keeps a laser-sharp focus on its **objectives**. For example, if a customer suggests a new feature or solution that doesn't contribute to the **objectives**, the team responds with a definite and non-negotiable no.

Visual example of OKRs from eyewear e-commerce company eyerim[56]

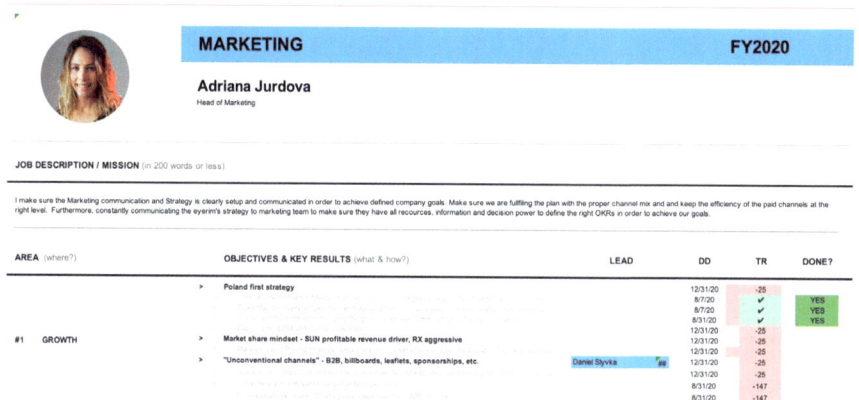

"THE ONLY SELF MANAGEMENT PROGRAM THAT WORKS IN THE ENTIRE WORLD IS THAT YOU DO A DAILY TO-DO LIST AT THE BEGINNING OF THE DAY, AND YOU REVIEW IT AT THE END OF THE DAY. THE REST YOU CAN EITHER

56   eyerim is the fastest-growing eyewear e-commerce company in Central and Eastern Europe.

CALL IT CUSTOMIZABLE OR BULLSH*T...

I THINK MEDITATION IS GREAT, SOFTWARE IS GREAT, TOOLS ARE GREAT. BUT NOTHING WORKS UNLESS YOU MANAGE IT. SOFTWARE IS ONLY AS GOOD AS THE HUMAN-WARE."

*- **Mark Harrison**, founder & CEO of **The T1 Agency**[57]*

The PERFORM Planning Method (PPM)

PPM, which has been used by hundreds of entrepreneurs, is a simple method based on years of research of some of the most effective productivity systems.[58]
Initially, it may seem like a lot of work, but it will soon become a quick and easy habit.

The example below explores how you can **use PPM to plan your day**, but you can apply the method to longer time periods as well.
We will use an example by **Viktoriya Vasilenko,** founder & CEO of

---

57   The T1 Agency is an integrated-experience agency based in Toronto, Canada.
58   PPM is inspired by the works of David Allen (Getting Things Done), Tim Ferriss (The 4 Hour Workweek), Tony Robbins (Time of Your Life), Brian Tracy, Peter Bregmann and other productivity experts.

KnowledgeGateGroup[59], who uses PPM to stay on top of things.

Step 1: Capture
What should you do tomorrow?
Take a look at your weekly goals, your projects, your meetings and commitments and capture everything you might need to get done.

1. CAPTURE
Create new job posting
Create and send contract for new hire
Make slides for new sales presentation
Revamp LinkedIn page
Follow up with leads
Go through game plan with sales team
Interview candidates
Find new office space
Follow up with accountant
Team meeting about remote work
Award interview
Sales meeting

59 Knowledge Gate Group is a Danish startup specialised in connecting companies to industry experts for micro-consultations.

Step 2: Group things together

Look closely at your list and group things together by project or area.

2. GROUP THINGS TOGETHER
Sales
Sales meeting
Follow up with leads
Go through game plan with sales team
Make slides for new sales presentation
Revamp LinkedIn page
Team
Team meeting about remote work
Create and send contract for new hire
Create new job posting
Interview candidates
Find new office space
CEO Duties
Award interview
Follow up with accountant

Step 3: Define the outcomes and action steps

3.1. Define the outcomes
For each of the groups, define the exact outcome you are trying to achieve.

3.2. Clarify the action steps
For each outcome you commit to, brainstorm what actions will help you achieve them.

3. DEFINE THE OUTCOMES AND ACTION STEPS

Grow customer base

Follow up with leads, ensure sales team is doing the same

Sales meeting - share learning from it

Go through game plan with sales team, ensure everyone is on the same page

Make slides for new sales presentation- ensure it is highly targeted

Revamp LinkedIn page with targeted customer base in mind

Grow team and ensure company culture is cultivated

Team meeting about remote work

Create and send contract for new hire

Create new job posting

Interview candidates

Find new office space

Ensure my duties are done to the utmost

Award interview - this is a marketing event, come prepared fully

Follow up with accountant

Step 4: Prioritise and delegate – your daily menu

When you go to a restaurant you have two choices:
a) order immediately
b) ask the waiter for a menu

If you choose option b, you will have to wait a few minutes before you can order. The advantage is that you can explore all the choices and know how much each item costs. This is exactly what you do at this step. You create your daily menu, with all the options and the actual **time cost** for each outcome and action step.

4.1. Define the priorities

Considering your lists of outcomes and action steps, decide which ones are:

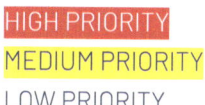

HIGH PRIORITY
MEDIUM PRIORITY
LOW PRIORITY

At this step you can use the Pareto Principle[60] or Eisenhower Matrix[61] to help you prioritise.

4.2. Estimate the time costs
Estimate how long it will take you to take each action step and achieve each outcome.

4.3. Delegate
Add the names of people to whom you can delegate some of your actions.

Delegate	Duration	Priority	Outcomes & Action Steps
			4. PRIORITIZE AND DELEGATE - YOUR DAILY MENU
			1. Grow customer base
	30m		Follow up with leads, ensure sales team is doing the same
	45 min		Sales meeting - share learning from it
	20 min		Go through game plan with sales team, ensure everyone is on the same page
Amro	1 hour		Make slides for new sales presentation- ensure it is highly targeted
Barney	45 min		Revamp LinkedIn page with targeted customer base in mind
	45 min		Meeting with a client
			2. Grow team and ensure company culture is cultivated
	30 min		Team meeting about remote work
Barney	45 min		Create and send contract for new hire
Barney	45 min		Create new job posting
	1 hour		Interview candidates
Viktor	1 hour		Find new office space
	15 min		Align with COO on strategy
			3. Ensure my duties are done to the utmost
	2 hours		Prepare well and do Award interview
	30 min		Follow up with accountant

Step 5: Schedule

Schedule your commitments in your calendar, starting by adding first the ones that are HIGH PRIORITY, then MEDIUM PRIORITY and finally if there is space left in your calendar - the LOW PRIORITY ones.

---

60   Pareto Principle states that roughly 20% of activities lead to 80% of the final results.
61   The Eisenhower Matrix is a tool that helps you to prioritise your tasks by urgency and importance.

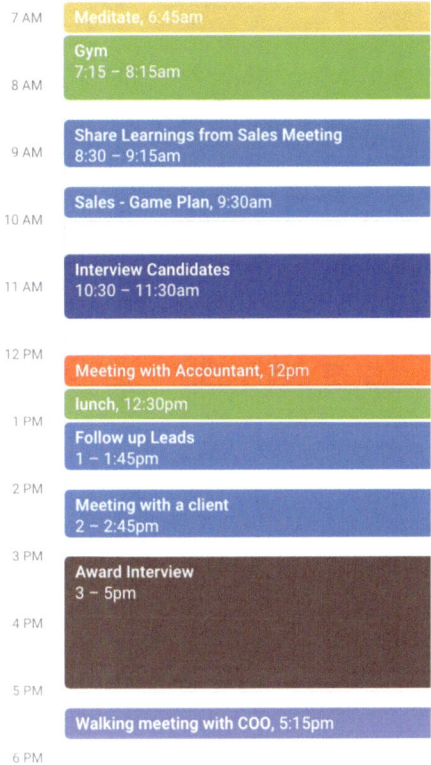

7 AM	Meditate, 6:45am
	Gym
8 AM	7:15 – 8:15am
9 AM	Share Learnings from Sales Meeting
	8:30 – 9:15am
10 AM	Sales - Game Plan, 9:30am
11 AM	Interview Candidates
	10:30 – 11:30am
12 PM	
	Meeting with Accountant, 12pm
1 PM	lunch, 12:30pm
	Follow up Leads
	1 – 1:45pm
2 PM	Meeting with a client
	2 – 2:45pm
3 PM	Award Interview
4 PM	3 – 5pm
5 PM	
	Walking meeting with COO, 5:15pm
6 PM	

A tip from Brian Tracy's time management book Eat the Frog is to schedule the tasks you really don't want to do (which are usually high impact) in the beginning of the day, when you're fresh and full of energy. The book is inspired by a quote from Mark Twain: "If it's your job to eat a frog, it's best to do it first thing in the morning. And If it's your job to eat two frogs, it's best to eat the biggest one first." Dealing with those tricky tasks builds momentum. Afterwards, everything comes easily.

KEY TAKEAWAYS

» By **planning effectively**, any founder can see the whole picture and maximize their limited startup resources

» The mindset of an Effective Planner has two elements
1) Outcome driven approach: Always start with the end in mind and build your action plan backwards
2) Adaptability and navigating change. Be nimble and ready to change the plan if the context changes

» **Aiming high** and setting goals accordingly can help you and your team focus on higher impact activities and help you reach further

» As a founder, it's your job to ensure **everyone in your team always knows your priorities**. Find your own system and make it consistent.

» Use the **Goals Pyramid** to help you to define the most important goal for a specific period and determine what has to happen to achieve it.

» **OKRs** is a very useful tool which maps:
1) Objectives, which are aspirational and provide direction
2) Key Results, which are measurable and concrete, outlining what it takes to reach the Objectives

» **The 5-Step PERFORM Planning Method (PPM)** helps you to organize your workflow effectively:
1) Capture
2) Group things together
3) Define outcomes and action steps
4) Prioritise and delegate
5) Schedule

ROLES & RESPONSIBILITIES

IN THIS CHAPTER, YOU WILL LEARN:

»   The difference between roles and responsibilities
»   The perfect set of roles for a founding team
»   How founding teams evolve: additional roles to consider early on
»   How responsibilities taken by each role can and will evolve over time
»   The need for both personal accountability, team responsibility and shared ownership
»   Methods for assigning responsibilities in the initial stages of a startup

"IT IS EASY TO DODGE OUR RESPONSIBILITIES, BUT WE CANNOT DODGE THE CONSEQUENCES OF DODGING OUR RESPONSIBILITIES."

- Josiah Charles Stamp[62]

---

62   Josiah Charles Stamp (1880 - 1941) was an English industrialist, economist, civil servant, statistician, writer, and banker. He was a director of the Bank of England and chairman of the London, Midland and Scottish Railway.

The difference between roles and responsibilities

Roles
The positions team members assume or the parts they play in a particular operation or process.

Responsibilities
The specific tasks or duties that team members are expected to complete as a function of their roles.

Both roles and responsibilities are important concepts for a startup to consider. Titles, however, matter less. It's understandable that founders choose ambitious titles to make a company look bigger and more important to external observers. It's important to remember that internally, in the day-to-day running of a startup, titles mean nothing.

What really matters is who is responsible for what tasks. A startup needs to determine how to best assign those responsibilities to the right team member, so the tasks get executed well and on time. When responsibilities are not clear, execution suffers: tasks progress slowly or are neglected. Consequently, the startup as a whole suffers and might even fail.

When assigning responsibilities, accountability also needs to be considered, as the two are inseparable. The main difference between responsibility and accountability is that responsibility can be shared while accountability cannot. If you are accountable, it means the buck stops with you. Someone else might be responsible for executing a task while you are accountable for it getting done. As the CEO, you are not only accountable for a multitude of tasks, but you need to make clear to your team which tasks you will carry out (take responsibility for) and which ones you can personally be held accountable for.

The lack of clear responsibilities and accountability is often the cause of tensions and disagreements within a startup management team. Nothing derails a startup faster than issues in the management team. In a study[63] of startup performance, venture capitalists attribute 65% of company failures to tension and problems arising within startup management teams.

Printify, the print-on-demand company you met in the Effective Planning chapter, found that lack of clearly assigned responsibilities inhibited growth, since it made it impossible to delegate tasks effectively. As the company grew, the co-founders understood that they needed to delegate more in order to give more power to the team. Initially, they did it without clearly defined roles and responsibilities. This created problems. People didn't know how to prioritise and struggled to complete tasks.

Realising what the issue was, the co-founders defined roles, responsibilities and accountability. This set the company on the right path. Printify now has a team of more than 100 people and much slicker operations. "The earlier you define the responsibilities under each role, the quicker you grow. " says Artis Kehris, Printify COO.

---

63   Source: Sahlman, W., Gorman, M. What Do Venture Capitalists Do? University of Illinois at Urbana-Champaign's Academy for Entrepreneurial Leadership Historical Research Reference in Entrepreneurship. 2009.

"THE EARLIER YOU DEFINE THE RESPONSIBILITIES UNDER EACH ROLE, THE QUICKER YOU GROW"

- Artis Kehris, Co-Founder & COO, Printify

Sometimes, friends or family co-found startups, as we saw with ZITICITY and Simporter. While this provides a great foundation for trust, it can make it harder for founders to demand accountability from each other. The key is to ensure that you have an objective way of measuring performance or evaluating how well tasks are carried out, even though this can be difficult.

Although it's important to assign personal responsibility and accountability for each task, in a startup you also have to foster a sense of shared ownership and responsibility. This means that each individual feels responsible for the success of the startup as a whole. A startup is no place for finger-pointing or passing the blame onto somebody else. Team members need to feel a sense of shared ownership of the entire enterprise and direction it is taking. This is most easily done by creating a culture of transparency, enabling everyone to ask for help. We'll discuss this in detail in the chapter on Robust Communication.

Cultural challenges in NewEurope

While it's essential to define roles and responsibilities, each person in a startup needs to acknowledge when they can't deliver something and ask for help. It's not unusual to run into big problems because people don't ask for help. In our work, we have seen this happen more often in NewEurope than anywhere else.

What we define as NewEurope is a large region with many different countries and cultures. They are not the same. Our experience has, however, led us to identify three factors that we believe are common and shape a culture of 'not asking for help' or waiting to do so until it's too late:

- In most of these countries, it feels unfair to others to ask for help. You should carry your own load.

- NewEurope has a culture of pride. People often think they have to deliver results no matter what. When they persist, they may fail. In a worst-case scenario, the company fails, too. The behaviour isn't bad in itself, but the attitude isn't helpful.

- People don't communicate enough. Sometimes a problem could be solved in 50 seconds if it was shared. By not talking about it, the problem often gets worse, until it's too late to do anything about it.

Being accountable in a responsible way means asking for help when you need it. Everyone struggles and fails sometimes. That's OK, as long as you are honest about it. It's much easier to be honest and speak up in an open culture of engagement and communication.

The perfect team of co-founders: size, roles and the 3Hs

Co-founders vs going solo - the perfect startup team size

Startup founder teams come in different shapes and sizes. We believe that it's not ideal to have only one founder. Paul Graham, co-founder of Y-Combinator, probably the world's best known and most successful accelerator, notes in his blog[64] that solo founders worry him: "What's wrong with having one founder is that it's a vote of no confidence. It probably means the founder couldn't talk any of his friends into starting the company with him. That's pretty alarming because his friends are the ones who know him best."

Just like Y-Combinator, SWG favours teams with several co-founders - ideally two or three. There is substantial evidence from market research that statistically, solo founders have a much harder journey. Across several cohorts of the most successful startup exits in the US, only 20% had solo founders.[65]

---

64   Source: Graham, P. The 18 Mistakes That Kill Startups, Paul Graham Blog, 2006.
65   Source: Hannah, J. (BetFair Founder and Early-Stage VC @ Matrix Partners) Analysis, How much more difficult is it to build a startup with a single founder versus having two founders?, Quora, 2011.
Retrieved from:
https://www.quora.com/How-much-more-difficult-is-it-to-build-a-startup-with-a-single-founder-versus-having-two-founders

"SOLO FOUNDERS, ON AVERAGE, TAKE 3.6 TIMES LONGER TO SCALE WHEN COMPARED TO STARTUP TEAMS OF TWO OR MORE."

– Startup Genome Report[66]

The investor view tends to be that having several co-founders reduces the risk of investment. If one founder quits, the others can pick up the load and won't send your investment down the drain. From the founders' point of view, the benefit of having several founders is a wider set of skills. Not a single person has all the necessary skills to get a venture going. Solo founders need to take many shortcuts.

Being a solo founder can also be tough. The entrepreneur journey is fun, but it's exceptionally demanding and full of ups and downs. The Through of Sorrow, a term coined by Paul Graham, is the period of struggle when a startup faces a setback. Having been there, Cristobal can confirm that it's a tough time. During those setbacks, co-founders help each other out of the hole.

"Great teams are the difference between quitting and deciding to go to battle one more time."
– Cap Watkins, Senior Product Design Manager at **Etsy**[67]

While we advise against launching a startup on your own, having more than four founders invites chaos. The more people involved, the harder it is to align and make critical decisions. Furthermore, in the long term,

---

66   Source: Chan, J. The Ultimate Guide To Creating the Perfect Founding Team, Foundr, 2019.
67   Etsy is an American e-commerce site focused
on handmade or vintage items and craft supplies

share of equity may become an issue: the more founders, the more ways the founder equity needs to be split.

The magic number seems to be between two and three founders. We tend to see three as ideal. If the roles (and related skills) are complementary, it also allows each role to be more specialised. This leads to better performance and greater efficiency. If the founders' skills are similar, two founders instead of three can allow greater trust and shared responsibility. All founders in a startup need to work well together and have a strong relationship.

"Startups do to the relationship between the founders what a dog does to a sock: if it can be pulled apart, it will be"[68]
- **Paul Graham**, American computer scientist, essayist, entrepreneur, venture capitalist, and author

Building a founder relationship on trust and respect: Zelos

Zelos[69] is an Estonian startup in the volunteer management space, providing a 'crucial task' delegation solution for volunteer teams. The company's co-founders are very different from each other, but over the years, they have proven to be a solid team, turning their differences into strengths.

Co-founders **Johanna-Mai Riisma** and **Viktor Lillemäe** have known each other for a long time. As teenagers, they even went to the same bar, although a four-year age difference meant they moved in different circles. They reconnected after bumping into each other in the same bar in 2014 and started working on what was to become Zelos in 2017.

Johanna highlights two reasons why they work well together: trust and shared values. When talking about building trust, they emphasize the importance of mutual understanding, focus on

---

68   Source: Graham, P. What we look for in founders, Paul Graham Blog, 2010.
69   Zelos won the Nordic Angel Program by Estonian Business Angel syndicate at Latitude 59 in 2019. More information at getzelos.com.

the Zelos vision and respect. "I'm proud that we try to take the time to understand the reasoning behind the choices the other makes," says Johanna. She notes that you need to respect your co-founder's expertise and trust that they also always have the startup's best interest in mind.

During the coronavirus pandemic in 2020, Zelos has been helping many volunteers across countries coordinate their efforts assisting senior citizens in need.

Roles and responsibilities within the ideal co-founder team

The ideal founding team covers the most critical roles and responsibilities. One of the most popular labels this ideal team has been given in startup literature is the 3H[70]: The Hustler, the Hacker and the Hipster. Drawing on these well-known terms, we have developed our own terminology: The Head, the Hand and the Heart. We wanted to use terms that better reflected the key skills needed to kick start a company: the ability to device, execute and communicate strategy, plans and targets.

The Head (The Hustler) needs to be both a visionary and a tireless salesperson.

As a visionary, the Head has the ability to unite and inspire the team. They see solutions where others see problems. As a salesperson, they don't stop until the customer says yes. The person taking on the role may be either more of a visionary or a salesperson when they start, but they need to develop the other skills to succeed, unless another founder takes on these tasks.

The Head also needs to cover another vital role: getting direct product feedback from the customers they meet. The Head must listen to the customer and share this feedback with the team as objectively as possible. This is essential to creating a product that will sell.

According to US serial entrepreneur David Cummings, "The [Head] is

---

70   Source: Cummings, D. Founding Team 3H: Hustler, Hacker, and Hipster. David Cummings Blog, 2018. Retrieved from: https://davidcummings.org/2018/02/28/founding-team-3h-hustler-hacker-and-hipster/

typically the leader [...] Someone has to make the key decisions, and one of the founders must be in charge".

"For your startup to succeed, you need someone who can pinpoint problems and articulate solutions. Every company encounters roadblocks. To keep your dream intact, you need someone with a way with words. Someone who can ground your mission in a path to success."
- Kalman Victor, CPO and co-founder of **Research Connection**

The Hand (The Hacker) is the person who can build the product and will develop the Minimum Viable Product from scratch. Hopefully, they can continue to develop a full product. (We will discuss this later in this chapter). The Hand needs to be able to translate the Head's vision into a product concept. As customer feedback arrives, they should improve the product accordingly, and add new product functionalities. The Hand is the person most under pressure at the initial stage of the company. Without the Hand, there is no product.

The Heart (The Hipster) is the customer experience (CX) and user interface (UI) expert who wants to delight the customer through every product and company interaction. The role combines a knack for both beauty and usability. Sometimes their desire to execute well comes into conflict with the Head's willingness to do it fast.
The Heart is the go-to person for any marketing and brand materials as well as content development, including the website and social media. For the product, the Heart should also be able to create visual product concepts and wireframes. The Heart is in the middle, translating customer feedback from the Head to the Hand and getting it incorporated into the product.

THE **3Hs** FOR A STARTUP TEAM

HACKER   **HIPSTER**   **HUSTLER**

THE HAND   THE HEART   THE HEAD

An alternative to the 3Hs: Roles and responsibilities at **Fractory**

The 3Hs is an ideal scenario, but what's important is that your team of founders cover these essential skill sets. Fractory, a B2B Industry 4.0 startup originally from Estonia, has three founders. This founding team is an example of a slightly different, but very successful, line-up. .In less than 3 years, Fractory has reached 300 customers and established a presence in the US and the UK.

Martin Vares, CEO of Fractory, explains that for the founding team, a clear split of responsibilities came quite naturally. They all have different backgrounds and each of their skill sets played an essential part of the business they were about to build.

Rein Torn had a software development background, so he was an obvious choice for CTO. For the other two roles the split diverges from the 3Hs. Joosep Merelaht had sales experience, but was simultaneously very down to earth and structured. This made him the ideal person to lead on everything relating to client conversion and later taking the helm of the sales team. Someone had to be the CEO and Martin didn't have a clear role. "For me, it wasn't too clear on paper why I should be the CEO (or as I called it, Chief Everything Officer) and at the same time there was no reason why I shouldn't be", explains Vares. "I was the one to push everything from the beginning." His persistence was evident as he didn't let go of the team's goals. "As time passed, I showed my ability to adjust and learn fast," he adds. "So I guess I earned my stripes." Vares also stresses that the founders were clear from the start that they would never resort to micromanagement. By clearly assigning responsibilities, they've made sure they've never needed to consider it.

Growing the team

Adding the Handler

From the perfect team of founders, there are several possible evolutions when the needs of the startup evolve. The need for additional skills can arise quickly. Analysis[71] from the Wesley Clover Innovation Center (WCIC.tech) found that a mere 6 months into the startup journey, many founding teams struggle to find direction. They grapple to accurately roadmap and efficiently develop their products. This often happens when the Heart is a designer and less of a product person. The seniority of the Hand also plays a part. Most senior developers have a good understanding of the principles of product development, while junior developers are often focused only on coding.

At SWG, we have seen this pattern repeated in several of our portfolio companies. In this situation, WCIC.tech recommends adding a fourth person to form what it calls the Startup Square.

---

71   Source: WCIC. Tech. How to Build a Startup Team Using a Startup Square, n.d.
Retrieved from: https://wcic.tech/build-a-startup-team-using-a-startup-square/

It labels this role **The Handler.**
The role depends on the strengths of the three co-founders. Often, the Handler needs to take responsibility for product management. The Handler frequently helps reconcile three competing demands: the Head wants to get a product to market quickly, the Heart seeks to ensure it has exceptional design and UI, and the Hand is a great developer but fails to plan the execution. Therefore, Handlers are typically involved in strategy, implementation and adaptation.They guide product development. "Always with the vision in mind, the product development will bring new product features, designs and strategy, all formulated around timetables, roadmap, pricing and specifications to ensure their validity to the vision," notes WCIC.Tech.
Good product managers are very hard to find, as they're often working for big companies. Expect to spend a long time recruiting for this role. If you find a good product manager, don't let them go. They'll be worth the money. Link them to the future success of the company through shares or ESOP (employee stock ownership) schemes.

Other vital roles to hire early

In the past year, we have held many workshops on roles and responsibilities. When we meet experienced and serial entrepreneurs, who have scaled their businesses from 20 to 100 employees, we always ask the same question: With hindsight, which role did you wish you had hired earlier?
At the INSEAD Entrepreneurship Forum in Barcelona in 2018, Cristobal discussed this with two very experienced and successful entrepreneurs: **Martins Sulte,** CEO and Co-founder of Mintos, one of NewEurope's hottest fintechs, and **Bart Huisken**, serial entrepreneur, who among other companies grew SouthWing[72], an early leader in Bluetooth headsets, to 45 people with sales channels in 20 countries and over $17 million in revenues. The situations we discussed differed, but three functional roles or areas emerged as crucial when a startup begins to scale:

---

72 Southwing is a VC funded pioneer and visionary leader of Bluetooth Mono and Stereo Wireless Headsets, Car kits and Speakers with a global team of 45 people, having sales channels in 20 countries and over 17M$ in revenues.

1. Chief Financial Officer (CFO) or a financial manager, depending on seniority. The rule of thumb is to hire this person either when you reach €10,000-15,000 monthly company costs and/or when you have money coming in and out from at least two different countries.

2. Chief Sales Officer (CSO) or a head of sales. In the early days, the CEO often handles sales, or a startup may hire a salesperson. But there comes a point when you need to scale sales and it often needs to happen quickly. You need someone to lead this process and your salesperson may not be a sales lead. For further insight on scaling your sales department, we recommend The Sales Acceleration Formula[73] by Mark Roberge, SVP of Worldwide Sales and Services for software company HubSpot. His insights are priceless, but also practical. Pay attention to the section on onboarding. It's an often overlooked part of the process, but perhaps the most important.

3. Chief Human Resources Officer (CHRO), Head of HR, or an HR person. This position relieves the founders of the task of recruitment and other HR processes. A rule of thumb is that if you hire three to four new people every quarter (and hiring is only a part of the HR and talent management job), you need an HR person. They will free up time for management to focus on driving company growth, but HR is also a vital part of the overall scaling process. Apart from hiring, HR plays an essential role in setting and maintaining company culture.

How roles evolve over time

Setting reporting expectations

As a startup grows, reporting lines will evolve. This is natural but can present challenges. Most of a startup's initial recruits report directly

---

73   Source: Roberge, M. The Sales Acceleration Formula: Using Data, Technology, and Inbound Selling to go from $0 to $100 Million, Wiley, 2015.

to the CEO or one of the co-founders. To many, this is one of the attractions of the job. There's a limit to how many direct reports one person can have, however. As the team grows, you may need to add a layer between the management team and some of those initial hires. To avoid disappointing them, be proactive and have that conversation up front.

Managing the challenges of role evolution

Roles and responsibilities will also evolve - including the duties you have as a founder. While many founders have great ideas and the drive to fuel startup success, they may be less capable of managing a growing organisation. As a founder, it can be challenging to acknowledge that you need to hire your own boss: someone with excellent management skills and a proven track record. This is a subject that deserves a separate book[74]. Psychologically, it can be hard for a founding CEO to remain in the company through this kind of shift in reporting structure. As the company grows, the Head or CEO dedicates more time to the company vision and growth, focusing less on the product. The Handler may over time become the Chief Product Officer (CPO), which is a crucial role as a startup scales. Working alongside the CEO, the CPO becomes the translator or mediator between marketing, sales and the development teams. They determine and define the product strategy - what features to build, at what time and at what cost. The CEO executes the company's vision, aligning the direction with the CPO and their vision for the product.

The evolution of the Hand or CTO role

To illustrate how roles change and evolve, we'll consider the evolution of the Hand in more detail. As the Hand sometimes takes on the CTO role, or leads the development team from the start, they are a potential CTO in the making. "The CTO Founder Triangle"[75] (see figure below) defines 3 main skills needed in a founder CTO: Engineering Manager,

---

74   The hiring of a CEO to manage co-founders often results in a power-struggle if the founder(s) remain significant shareholders. This deserves its own book.

75   Source: Ariav, Y. (VC, Founder @ Fundbox, Product chief @ Onavo (acq. Facebook)). How do you view the role of CTO at an early stage startup? Quora, 2017.

Product Leader and Chief Wizard (a person with an innate talent for coding and tech tools). All genuinely great CTOs should have at least a basic grasp of all three areas, while excelling at two of them.

Pat Kua, a seasoned technology lead, who is CTO and Chief Scientist at N26, Europe's leading and most valuable neobank[76], puts it differently: He lists leadership, development and architecture as the core skills of a technology leader. [77]

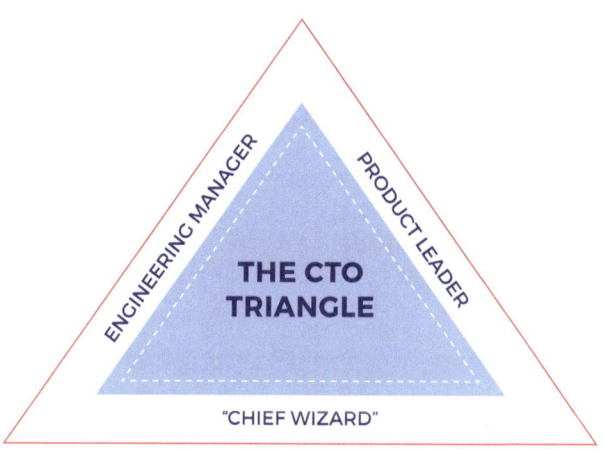

The responsibilities of the CTO role changes significantly over time, however (see fig.). At the initial business ideation stage, the CTO is assessing the technical feasibility and innovation potential, acting as a product leader. Once the idea has taken shape, the CTO develops the architecture and the infrastructure of the company (Engineering manager) and develops the initial MVP and product versions (Chief Wizard) . However, when we reach the product-market fit, the CTO needs to manage the infrastructure, ensure the security of the product and develop their team's engineering and development culture.

76   A neobank is an online-only bank. N26 has a valuation of €3.5 billion.
77   Source: Pat Kua. The Definition of a Tech Lead, 2020.
      Retrieved from: https://www.patkua.com/blog/the-definition-of-a-tech-lead/

Applying a long term vision: Vinted

Mindaugas Mozuras has evolved from software engineer into the lead of Engineering at Vinted, Lithuania's first unicorn and an accomplished blogger[78]. Vinted's mission is to make second-hand the first choice worldwide. His team in the engineering department supports Vinted's long term vision, applying what he defines as Sustainable Speed. They use Lean Software Development principles[79] to achieve this.

"We want Vinted to succeed long-term. We have long-term ambitions," explained Mindaugas. "We don't want to move with limitations. We don't want bugs and debt, which we'll have to fix a year from now. We don't want unhappy people who leave. We want the opposite of short-term aspirations. We want to grow at a sustainable speed. We're even willing to sacrifice speed today to be faster long-term. We want to deliver value to our members fast, and even faster a year from now."

78   Mozuras, M., How We Approach Engineering At Vinted, 2018.
Retrieved from:http://engineering.vinted.com/2018/09/04/how-we-approach-engineering-at-vinted/
79   More information: Poppendieck, M., Poppendieck, T. Lean Software Development: An Agile Toolkit, can be accessed at http://www.poppendieck.com/

WHAT IS THE ROLE OF A CTO THROUGHOUT THE STARTUP LIFECYCLE?

STAGE	CTO FOCUS AREAS
1 BUSINESS IDEA	Assessing Technical Feasibility
	Developing MVP
2 EARLY STAGE STARTUP	Inventing
	Designing the app architecture
	Setting up the app infrastructure
3 REACHING PRODUCT-MARKET FIT	Infrastructure management
	Ensuring security of the product
	Building a coding culture
4 GROWTH	Developing the product vision
	Launching new product lines
	Ensuring competitive advantage with the help of cutting edge technology

As a startup grows, the CTO role needs to shift. The CTO should develop the product vision, launch new product lines and use cutting edge technology to ensure the product has competitive advantage. This means the role leaves behind the "Chief Wizard" aspect and starts concentrating more on product development (until a CPO is in place). Increasingly, the CTO role demands an engineering-development manager.

To successfully move between the responsibilities at each stage, a CTO needs to both have the right skills to do so and be flexible and happy to meet these different demands. A significant risk in this journey is that the CTO loses interest in the task at hand. A true innovator may not be passionate about managing infrastructure on a day to day basis, for example. To do an excellent job in the high-pressure startup environment, passion is paramount. If you are a CTO, make sure you ask yourself what you like doing and not. Hand over responsibility for the tasks that don't fit you and focus on what you do best and enjoy doing.

Working at the intersection of your strengths and passions

The evolution of responsibilities as a startup grows is not limited to the CTO role. The responsibilities of each co-founder and manager in the business will need to be continuously evaluated.

When leaders manage people's strengths and passions well on an ongoing basis, you will eventually find your team working in "The Zone". This is the territory where magic happens on a personal, employee and co-founder level. If you want to build a peak-performing team, create an organisation where people love what they do. Enable them to spend the majority of their time on activities and projects they are passionate about.

After all, what's the point of working in a startup that is high risk and requires long hours of stressful work, if you're not spending most of your time on what you love doing? Furthermore, a startup is more likely to get investment if the team is passionate about what it does. Imagine two teams that are equally skilled. One has passion and the other is primarily focused on profit. Which one would you invest in?

The exercise below will help you assign roles and responsibilities to harness both passion and strengths.

**STRENGTHS &
PASSIONS**

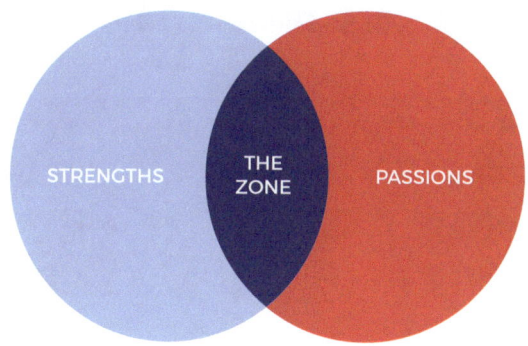

Exercise: Map of Responsibilities - Doing what you do best vs doing what you love

Our workshops always include this exercise, inspired by Eric Edmeades[80]. It helps map the level of skill and passion for each of the responsibilities assigned to team members, allowing you to identify areas where responsibilities need to be changed. Founders who have worked together for years and are very clear on one another's strengths often discover new, subtle aspects of what others love doing. Using a simple spreadsheet is a great way to start this exercise.

---

80   Eric Edmeades is a Canadian serial entrepreneur and professional speaker. He is also the founder of Business Freedom Academy. Role-Mapping is an exercise originally developed by Eric Edmeades to help entrepreneurs achieve business freedom. The exercise in the PERFORM book is an adaptation of Mr. Edmeades' work.

MAP OF
RESPONSIBILITIES

List all your responsibilities and mark with a different colour how you feel about each of them with respect to your strengths and passions.

Step 1: Everyone in the team individually writes down a list of every responsibility they have or might have in the company.

Step 2: Everyone in the team individually highlights how they feel about each responsibility.
Green: Things you are good at **and** passionate about: **THE ZONE**
Yellow: Things you are reasonably good at, but not very passionate about: **OK**
Red: Things you hate doing or you aren't very good at: **NEEDS CHANGE**

Step 3: Look at the results as a team and discuss:
- Can you switch any responsibilities between team members?
- Are there any areas everyone marks with RED (NEEDS CHANGE)?
- What does this mean when it comes to your next hire?

Step 4: Commit to specific action steps.
Define concrete action steps to improve your team's allocation of responsibilities.

The following is an example of this exercise Stoyan did with his COO - Annija Matisone and Marketing Assistant - Marija Gracova.

Responsibility	CEO	COO	Marketing Assistant
Finance, Legal, Admin			
Book-keeping			
Budgeting & Finance			
Contracting			
Operations & Management			
Strategy & Vision			
Project Management			
Team Lead			
Recruitment & HR			
Pre-screening Candidates			
Interviewing			
Onboarding			
Sales			
Networking & Lead Gen			
Cold Calling			
Negotiation & Closing Deals			
Marketing			
Research & Benchmark			
Idea Generation			
Social Media Management			
Digital Marketing & Content Creation			
Copywriting & Proofreading			
Customer Service			
Communication & Coordination			
Customer Support			

Doing the exercise together and discussing the results helped the team to understand each other better and make adjustments to the responsibilities each team member owns.

The RACI-matrix[81]: assigning responsibility and accountability

"If you don't have the right people for right responsibilities, you will have a detrimental effect"
- **Anders Thomsen**, CEO of **no-more**[82]

---

81   RACI which is what you'll find in Project Management Institute (PMI)'s PMBOK for project management. There is another version called DARCI. RACI is the same as DARCI but excludes the Decision-Maker and we find it with a more extensive usage.
82   no-more is a Danish b2b service company specialised in ad hoc outsourcing.

R RESPONSIBLE	Who will be doing this task? Who is assigned to work on it?
A ACCOUNTABLE	Who has the authority to take decisions? Who will ensure delivery on time and to the right level of quality?
C CONSULTED	Who can give me information to complete the task better? Any stakeholders already identified?
I INFORMED	Whose work depends on this task? Who has to be kept updated about progress?

RACI is a tool that complements the Map of Responsibilities exercise. It creates greater clarity around who-does-what for each task. The acronym stands for Responsible, Accountable, Consulted and Informed.

Responsible: The person who will actually get it done. There can be more than one responsible person for each task or project.

Accountable: This is where the buck stops. The person who is accountable will ensure delivery on time and to the right level of quality. If something goes wrong, they need to be able to explain what happened and how it will be fixed. A person may be both responsible and accountable for a task, but accountability can only fall to one individual.

Consulted: Who can give me information to complete the assignment better? Who should I consult before making a major decision?

Informed: Whose work depends on this task? Who has to be updated about progress?

The framework can be used for specific projects or tasks, but it can also provide the foundation for everything you do[83]. For example, **Thibaut Taittinger,** co-founder and CEO of Puzl CowOrKing, the largest provider of co-working spaces in the Balkans, grew his company to 600+ tenants by using the RACI Matrix to assign responsibilities and delegate tasks to his team.

RACI helps engage people in a discussion around roles and responsibilities. It is important to review the matrix continuously. In a project, you may review responsibilities after each stage. If you use RACIs to map responsibilities in the initial stages of your startup, review them at least once a quarter to make sure they are still valid. If somebody has responsibilities they're not fulfilling, you can address it. Why is it not working and what actions should be taken? Perhaps the person is not the best sales manager, but he or she is excellent at another role. Shuffle the roles and responsibilities to solve the problem.

During the second week of each Startup Wise Guys batch[84], we run the PERFORM workshop with 10-12 startups and go through most of the content and exercises in this book. We always ask the startups to draw up a RACI-matrix. Co-founders often discover that they hadn't been clear over who was doing what. Below is an example of one of our startups - Moduulo[85], with three co-founders and one developer. After the exercise, it became clear that they needed to hire two additional roles to get to the next stage.

---

83   Although the RACI was initially developed for specific projects, we believe that on the initial stages of a startup, it can be applied to the entire startup
84   SWG invests together in 10/12 startups and brings them as a batch to work together full time and combining online and onsite for up to 5 months .
85   Moduulo is and Estonian startup focused on smart invoicing.

RACI-Matrix of Moduulo

Sector	Activity	CEO	CTO	CAO	Dev	CMO (to be hired)	BizDev (to be hired)
Marketing	Planning / Strategy	A,R	C	C	C	C	C
	Content Production	C		A		R	
	Social Media	C		A		R	I
	Design & Layout	C		A,R		R	I
	Public Relations PR	A,R	R	R		R	R
Sales	Planning / Management	A,R					
	Business Development	A,R	C	I		I	R
	Key Account Management	A,R	I			I	
	Sales	A,R	R	R	R	R	R
	Lead Generation	A,R	R	R	R	R	R
Technology	Product Development	C	A,R		R		
	Tech Management	C	A,R				
	Development & Onboarding	I	A,R		R		
	Customer Care	I	A,R		R		
	Process Specialist	I	A,R		R		
HR	Planning of ressources	A,R	C				
	Recruiting / Hiring	A,R	C				
Finance	Planning	A,R					
	Accounting	I		A			
	Controlling	A,R					
	Fundraising	A,R	C	C			
Adminstration	Legal & Admin	I		A,R			

KEY TAKEAWAYS

» **Roles and responsibilities are important** for a startup: Consider who is responsible for which tasks and how you best assign responsibilities. **Titles matter less.**

» **Responsibility and accountability** are inseparable. Responsibility can be shared but accountability cannot.

» Each person in a startup needs to acknowledge when they can't do something and ask for help. It's common to run into problems because people don't **ask for help**.

» Having one founder is not ideal. The magic number is between two and three founders, covering the most critical roles and responsibilities: **The Head, the Hand and the Heart.**

» The next key role to recruit is **the Handler**. Handlers are typically involved in strategy, implementation and product adaptation.

» Other roles to add when you are scaling are: **Chief Financial Officer (CFO)** or a financial manager, **Chief Sales Officer (CSO)** or head of sales and the **Chief Human Resources Officer (CHRO)** or Head of HR

» **Set reporting expectations.** As the team grows, you may need to add a layer between the management team and some of the initial hires. To avoid disappointing them, be proactive and have that conversation up front.

» **Continuously evaluate** the needs and **responsibilities of each person and role**. To build a peak-performing team, create an organisation where people love what they do and spend the majority of their time on activities and projects they are passionate about (In The Zone)

FOCUS & EXECUTION

IN THIS CHAPTER YOU WILL LEARN:

» How to navigate a world of distractions
» Why you should raise your standards of execution
» How successful founders step up Focus & Execution
» Three Lessons to help you level up your Focus & Execution
» To recognize the five villains stealing your Focus & Execution and how to beat them

"THE SUCCESSFUL WARRIOR IS THE AVERAGE MAN, WITH LASER-LIKE FOCUS."

- Bruce Lee[86]

---

86   Bruce Lee (1940 - 1973) was a Hong Kong American actor, director, martial artist, martial arts instructor and philosopher.

Navigating a world of distraction

Focus
The main or central point of attention or interest

Execution
The carrying out of a plan, an order or a course of action

In the first three chapters, we explored the importance of setting a strong basis for a productive culture. You define your purpose, vision and values, create clarity around the roles and responsibilities in the team and adopt an outcome-driven mindset where consistent planning is a priority. But even if you master all this, nothing will get done unless you execute. Every day, you need to be relentless in your **execution**, to produce results in the core **focus** areas you have defined.

It's more difficult than ever to stay focused. We simply have too many choices and possibilities. Choice abounds not only in terms of the product features to build and the customer segments to target through a startup, but in the life of a founder overall, such as where to live, whom to date and how to spend free time.

It's easy to get distracted. We have mobile computers in our pockets. Using your smartphone, you can download billions of applications, consume limitless content and buy anything you can think of in just a few clicks. We're addicted to technology. If you're checking your phone in the first 15 minutes after waking up, you're just like 80% of all humans. According to a study,[87] we spend 3 hours and 15 minutes a day on our smartphones.

We switch between computer applications around 600 times a day. We check our emails more than 11 times an hour. A Harvard study[88] found that we spend 47% of our waking hours thinking about something other

---

[87] Source: MacKay, J. Screen time stats 2019: Here's how much you use your phone during the workday, RescueTime, 2019.
[88] Source: Killingsworth, M. A., Gilbert, D. T. A Wandering Mind is an Unhappy Mind, Science, November 12, 2010.

than what we're doing.

Think about all the hours of lost productivity. You have no time to lose: You need to cut out the distractions. With less than 10% startup survival rate,[89] you should be conscious about every minute and invest it carefully in activities that bring results.

Focus and execution are closely linked and both crucial to master as an entrepreneur. This chapter teaches you how to smoothly and efficiently turn your plans and goals into results.

Raising your standard of execution

No one built a great company with a great idea but mediocre execution. Conversely, if you have a reasonable idea and a committed team with a tenacious spirit, you have a much greater chance of success. The higher your standards of execution, the better you become at understanding what works and what doesn't and where should your focus go.

It's worth remembering that it often takes a lot more effort than we expect to achieve results. Stoyan is a co-founder and partner in a company for high-end mastermind[90] experiences and business retreats: Samodiva Masterminds. When Samidova launched its first product, a seven-day mastermind retreat, the team had only two months to sell the tickets.

Stoyan thought the places would get filled easily. After all, the team had designed an amazing product, an experience they themselves would have jumped on the chance to attend. They had invited international speakers, booked 5-star hotels and combined adventures and fun activities with in-depth personal growth sessions and workshops, all at a reasonable price.So why wouldn't people pay for it?

As no bookings came in during the first few weeks, they had to face the

---

89   Source: https://startupgenome.com/reports/gser2020, see footnote 8.
90   Masterminding is a peer-to-peer learning format used for generating ideas, exploring and solving personal or business challenges.

facts: they had dropped the ball when it came to marketing. **No one knew what the event was and why they should care.**

Due to the short deadline, pre-payment had been required for most of the logistics. That investment was at stake. The team had a deadline and a clear goal: **"Attract 12 quality participants to the retreat".** There was no time to lose.

During the remaining weeks, Stoyan personally reached out to more than 1,400 people from his network, talking about the event, inviting them to participate and asking for feedback and referrals. He ran online campaigns. He was obsessed. He used any opportunity to reach the goal, working every minute of the day. These were some of the most hectic weeks he'd ever lived through. It was intense, but it paid off. Samodiva managed to attract 12 quality participants[91] for the retreat and had a great proof of concept.

Three key lessons came out of this experience:

Lesson 1: The fewer the priorities, the better the focus

For two months, Stoyan had one major goal, clearly defined and sealed with a deadline. Since his attention wasn't scattered in different directions, it was easier to build momentum and achieve the goal.

No more than three: Focus at Circle

"As a founder you need to learn to focus," stresses **Melissa Rosenthal**, co-founder at SMS-tech platform Circle and former Executive Vice President at Buzzfeed. "At any given time in your startup you only have two or three things you should really focus on.

At Circle, at the moment they are:
1. Making the product the best it can be
2. Understanding how the users are using it and iterating accordingly
3. Customer acquisition

---

91   In the end, one of the participants didn't join due to complications with a visa.

We have plenty of ideas and plans on what we should do in the future. But right now, we know we should stay focused."

Lesson 2: You are probably under-executing! Step up your game

Once the retreat was over, the first thing Stoyan thought was: **"How can I apply a similar level of commitment and execution to my day-to-day projects and activities?"**
When you have an ambitious goal, a clear action plan and strong motivation to follow through, you can produce a lot more than you imagine. You have to raise your standards of execution, though. In the chapter on Effective planning we discussed the importance of multiplying your goals by ten. To achieve great results, you need to put in a lot of effort. This starts with a mindset shift.

Boris Krastev and Boris Borisov, CEO & CPO of **RemoteMore**, are great examples of founders with high standards of execution. Stoyan was coaching them in the early stages of their startup.
When they built their first prototype, they wanted to validate the market for it. They made a list of 300 leads and cold-called them within the next three days.This is one of numerous cases where founders define clearly what they need to get done, set an ambitious and measurable outcome and apply laser focus to get it done.

Optimizing working hours: RemoteMore

RemoteMore is always trying to optimize its way of working to fuel long-term productivity, explains CEO **Boris Krastev**. "In the early days of the company we tested and experimented with an optimal working week in terms of hours for us," he says. "We tried different options, writing down a productivity score from 1 to 10 for each day. We found that our optimal number is 70 hours per week. Doing more than that was not sustainable for us and meant loss of productivity later."
As data-driven founders, they measure every hour they work.

> For the first 2.53 years (that's how precise they are!) the co-founders worked on average 72.1 hours per week, (excluding the two weeks' holiday they take each year). Since they make sure that time is productive, their output is correspondingly high.

Often founders under-execute, because they don't realize what they're capable of. Most founders we interviewed for this book know it's important to raise your standards of execution. You're able to produce so much more than you can imagine. A great hack you can use to step up your daily execution comes from entrepreneur Ed Myllet[92]. In a video[93] Myllet shares the concept of **6-hour days**.
Instead of planning for one day, he breaks 24 hours down into three:
Day 1: from 6am to 12noon
Day 2: from 12noon to 6pm
Day 3: from 6pm to midnight

This simple mindset shift allows him to stay focused and produce more than he would normally do, since he's driven by the time limit. What mindset shift do you need to make to raise your own standards of execution?

Lesson 3: Start speaking to customers as early as possible

Many startups have failed because they waited too long before talking to customers. They ended up **building products and features that the market didn't want**.
When Samodiva Masterminds planned its retreat, the team spoke to hundreds of customers before they developed their products. This allowed them to:
a) Validate that there was a market need
b) Define who the target customers were and what are their pain points

---

92   Ed Myllet is founder and Chairman of World Financial Group (WFG) and the host of The Ed Mylett Show.
93   Source: Ed Mylett. This is the GREATEST THING You Can Do Every Morning!, 2019. Retrieved from: https://youtu.be/dC67d0lzzAs

c) Refine the product, so it met customer needs

Speaking to potential customers also meant that when Stoyan started his blitz-like sales effort, he had warm leads to turn to. Connecting with customers for research helps you generate leads for the future.

Customer input helps you make the right pivot: Leanplum

Leanplum is a leading multi-channel customer engagement platform, which has raised more than $125 million. Early on, the company co-founders were intending to build a product **by engineers for engineers**. To test it, they talked to 200 engineers and realized those interested in the product were actually the product managers. They quickly pivoted and shifted the focus of the company.

Momchil Kyurkchiev, co-founder and CPO at Leanplum, said in an interview with TrendingTopics.eu that it was one of the most eye-opening experiences in his entrepreneurial journey. "One of my biggest fears when starting Leanplum was that we would build a company, start building a product, announce it and then nobody would use it. What I realized later was that if you actually talk to customers and you ask them what their biggest problems are, you can build a product that solves these problems. By definition there are going to be people who want it."

Sometimes founders are afraid of sharing their ideas because they're worried others will steal them. **Hedi Mardisoo**, founder & CEO of **Catchet**, an Estonian financial services marketplace for gig workers, urges other founders not to worry. "Many people can have the same idea, but the question is how you execute it," she says. "I was also scared to talk about my idea early on, but then I understood. I thought 'OK fine let them do it.' It's all about execution in the end. If you do it well, then you win. If not: be happy that the idea gets executed and seen by the world."

Where to focus

The more focused you are, the more momentum you will gain. However,when you're first starting up, you'll need to spread yourself a bit more. After all, you're the Chief Everything Officer.

Martin Zahuranec, founder & CEO of Slovakia-based **eyerim**, the fastest growing eyewear e-commerce company in CEE, says advice from the company's investment manager, **Elbruz Yilmaz**, has stuck with him: "When you are starting as a founder, you need to be a Swiss army knife. As your company grows, you need to be a Katana, that cuts only one way," Martin explains: "When you start as a founder, you have to do all kinds of things. In the early stages of **eyerim** for example, I was doing everything. I was spec-ing the packages, I was designing the email signature... at the same time I was pitching and negotiating marketing agency fees. Eventually, the shareholder structure and the business itself becomes so complex that you just need to focus. You can only do that by delegating; by purposely and consciously removing yourself from the processes."

Focus is paramount when it comes to your target market. Many startups try to be everything to everyone and fail because they don't provide a product that serves the need of a specific market. Instead of spreading yourself too thinly, spend time finding the customers who need your product. Understand this target market and build the product so that it serves these customers well. Focus all your efforts on that segment before scaling to the next.

Who will walk across broken glass?

Mick Lubinskas is a serial entrepreneur and investor who has built six products that generated more than $50 million in revenue, serving 50 million users. In a lecture[94], Lubinskas

---

94   Source: Liubinskas, M. On Focus, 2015. The video available at:
https://youtu.be/9eflivDMHa4

challenged founders to ask themselves a simple question to help define the customer segment they should focus on: "How can I find these people, who will walk across...broken glass to use my product?" He stressed the importance of keeping your focus rather than trying to be everything to everyone. "It's so easy to think the reason customers don't love you is that you need more features" he added. Don't fall into this trap.

Let's explore the villains that stand in the way of focus and execution, and how to deal with them.

The 5 villains of focus & execution

Villain 1: Lack of clear priorities

"Alice: Which way should I go?
Cat: That depends on where you are going.
Alice: I don't know.
Cat: Then it doesn't matter which way you go."
- Lewis Carroll, Alice in Wonderland

This villain can be a little invisible. Even if you're not clear what your priorities are, you might still be efficient and get a lot of things done. As we explored in the chapter on Effective planning, you might be under the illusion that you're productive just because you're busy. That's not necessarily true. When your priorities aren't set, it's likely you won't be as focused on the most important areas and suffer productivity cost. When the day hits you with all demands and requests a startup founder has to deal with, it's easy to switch on your reactive mode, giving your attention to 'what's screaming the loudest'.

How to beat Villain 1, Lack of Clear Priorities:
Get more clarity

We spent a whole chapter sharing ideas about how to plan effectively, so you always know what your priorities are. The same has to be true for your team. As a leader, you should be aware where the attention of your team is at any point and gently remind them if they veer off track.

Personal prioritization: Steli Efti from Close

Steli Efti is the co-founder & CEO of Close, a fully distributed sales automation CRM company for inside sales[95] teams. Steli is originally Greek, but grew up in Germany and successfully built Close, now headquartered in San Francisco but operating globally. He has developed his own method for allocating his time and focus: "When it comes to prioritization, obviously experience plays a role, but there are certain questions that can lead you to your priorities," he says. Steli asks himself: "What is something that I'm more qualified for than anybody else in the company, so when I do it, we make progress? What are the most important things that only I can do?". This creates specific areas of focus, he says. "For example, when it comes to hiring senior executives. That's something that I am the best person to do in the company. It takes a lot of time. It's very hard work. But it pays massive dividends for the company. There's almost nothing with higher leverage I can do."

On the other side of the equation are less demanding activities. "There are things that are good for the company that don't require much effort on my side, so I do them," he explains. "For two years I would record a 5-10 minute video every day for our YouTube channel. I would only spend 10 minutes on it." He would record a first cut, with no editing. The task was easy, but it brought significant value by fuelling visibility and bringing a personal touch to the brand. Steli points out that it wasn't his

---

95   "Inside sales means the sale of products or services by personnel who reach customers through phone, email, or the internet."
Source: Tarver, E. Inside Sales Definition, Investopedia, 2019. Retrieved from: https://www.investopedia.com/terms/i/inside-sales.asp

core priority, but with so little of his time needed, the cost vs return ratio was high.

Tools and ideas

1. Define your Vital Few

Ask yourself:

- If you had to spend 80% of your time in only three areas, which ones would they be?

- How much of your time do you spend on them today?

- What can you do to improve the percentage?

2. Block time daily for Effective Planning

Schedule up to 30 minutes in your calendar daily to have a look at your priorities and demands on your time. Define the core outcomes you are working towards[96].
Tools such as the PERFORM Planning Method from Chapter 2: Effective Planning can be useful.

3. Build the habit of daily team stand-ups

Keep it simple and to the point. A good agenda can look like this:
- Short **news and updates** from the CEO or manager
- Take turns to share **progress** from the previous day
- Take turns to share the **objectives** for the day
- Briefly share potential **challenges and struggles**

Defining your Vital Few: Federico Bortoletto from Oppi

Stoyan had a coaching session with one of his clients,

---

96   Use the tools in the Effective Planning chapter to help you.

Federico Bortoletto, an entrepreneur and founder of Oppi, a strategic change consultancy based in Denmark. Usually very enthusiastic, Federico sounded exhausted and stressed. He was overwhelmed. The business was taking off, but he had too much on his plate and it was difficult for him to navigate it all. On top of that, he had a young child, with a second one on the way.

During the session, Stoyan asked Federico to share his top three **Vital Few** areas. Federico admitted he was spending only 5-10% of his time on these key priorities, which should ideally occupy 70-80%. This realization made Federico look for ways to improve his time management. He concluded that he could afford hiring someone and delegate some of his responsibilities to her.

Only a few weeks later, he was already spending 70-80% on his top three **Vital Few areas** and feeling a lot more engaged and productive.

Villain 2: The "Shiny Object Syndrome"

"MY BIGGEST PRODUCTIVITY TOOL IS SAYING NO."

- Steli Efti, *co-founder and CEO,* **Close**

Even though you're clear over what your priorities are, you might still struggle to keep your focus on them.

Stoyan has a 10-month old niece. When she sees a new toy that makes sounds or flickers, she gets excited and goes after it. Once she finally gets it, she starts to lose interest. Her focus goes to the next shiny object. In the same way, entrepreneurs are often natural yes-sayers, who easily get motivated and excited. We come up with a brilliant new idea, marketing plan, product feature innovation or customer segment. We immediately connect the dots in our heads and envision the impact it can have. While this is the same spirit that pushes us forward, opening doors to new opportunities and directions, it can also have negative effects.

If you're constantly starting new things without considering why, you risk losing direction. You might not have the resources to follow through with the projects you've already started. In business, it tends to take time and consistent work to reach sustainable results.

"The shiny object syndrome" is well visualized in this graph by Jan Sullivan, CEO of Doodle Videos Made for You, an Australian video production company.

How to beat Villain 2, "Shiny Object Syndrome":
Learn to say no!

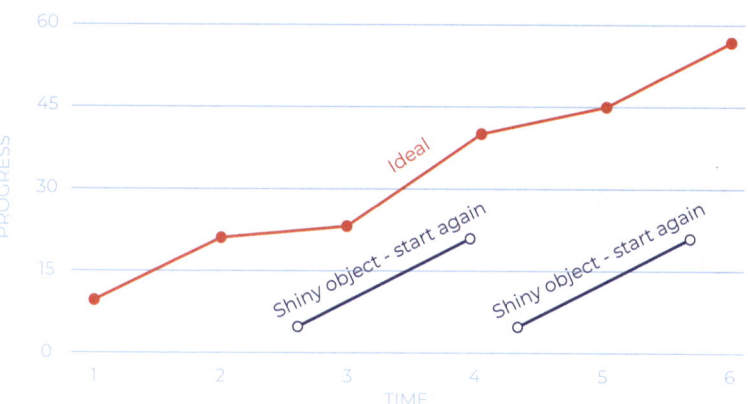

Tools and strategies

1. Take your time before you commit

We tend to say yes to new ideas and requests when we get excited. Instead, take your time before you respond. Come back to it the next day and see if it still seems relevant. Ask yourself: Why do you want to say yes? Is it worth the effort?

2. Calculate the opportunity cost

When we look at a new idea, request or project it's easy to focus only on the potential positives. Remember that whenever you say yes to something, you likely have to say no to something else. Create the habit of evaluating the opportunity cost. What do you need to let go of if you take on a new project?

3. Discuss new projects and commitments with your team before greenlighting them

Take new ideas to your co-founders and team to discuss and stress test them. Are they relevant, given your priorities and KPIs? What are the potential risks or downsides?

Villain 3: Procrastination

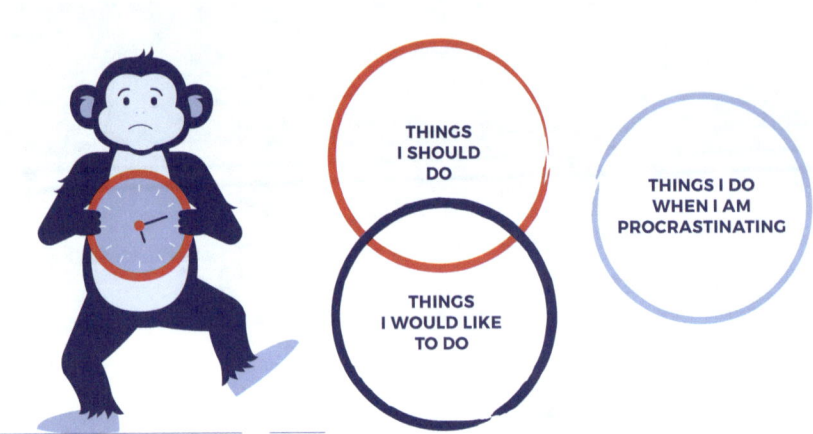

Procrastination comes from the Latin pro, meaning "forward, forth, or in favor of, " and crastinus, meaning "of tomorrow".The Cambridge Dictionary definition is:**"To keep delaying something that must be done, often because it is unpleasant or boring."** Procrastination is a huge productivity killer. According to a study[97] of 865 office workers, Brits procrastinate 122 minutes a day.

The question is not whether you procrastinate or not. Everyone procrastinates. The question is how **much you** procrastinate, and **do you understand where your procrastination comes from**? When you are aware of the origin, you have a better chance of taking ownership and decrease the time you procrastinate.

According to Leo Babauta, the author of the book Zen Habits, we

97   Source: Davies, T. Survey Reveals How Much Time We Really Waste In The Working Day, Rebootonline.com, 2017. Retrieved from: https://www.rebootonline.com/blog/survey-reveals-how-much-time-we-really-waste-in-the-working-day/

procrastinate because we fear discomfort or uncertainty. Babauta[98] suggests we avoid doing difficult tasks because we fear:

- That we don't know what we're doing

- That we're gonna mess up and look bad

- That we'll succeed and then have to face a scarier situation

- That the task will be difficult and uncomfortable

How to beat Villain 3, procrastination: Start doing!

Think about the last time you procrastinated on an important task. What was the reason? What can you do next time to beat this villain? In simple terms, beating procrastination means **motivating yourself to do what has to be done, regardless of whether you feel like it or not.**

Tools and ideas

1. Just start - and focus single-mindedly

Sometimes we procrastinate because we are too overwhelmed and don't know where to begin. You don't have to have it all figured out from the beginning. Try to break the task down into actionable sub-tasks. Then pick one and focus on it single-mindedly. By completing one task, you will gain momentum, which will motivate you to keep going.

2. Lower your expectations

If you feel really stuck, you might want to start by lowering your expectations. Many entrepreneurs and creative people apply this trick to beat procrastination. For example, we might have a daily target to write ten pages of good content for this book. Some days we're highly motivated and reach the goal. Other days, when we don't feel like it, a better strategy might be to aim for a single page. Once we start and get

---

98   Source: Babauta, L. A Guide to Overcoming Procrastination & Finding Focus, Zen Habits, n.d. Retrieved from: https://zenhabits.net/focusguide/

into the flow, we usually exceed the initial target.

3. Schedule time for purposeful procrastination

Explore what you usually do when you procrastinate. Do you enjoy doing those activities? You might want to schedule time when you procrastinate on purpose.

Stoyan recently mentored a startup founder from North Macedonia, who used to waste a lot of time procrastinating by playing video games. Sometimes he would play instead of working.

His solution was to block specific times in which he procrastinated on his own terms. That way he would control the time he spent on procrastination.When he feels like procrastinating during the day, he's able to quickly return to his core priorities, since he knows he'll be able to procrastinate on purpose later on.

Villain 4: Multitasking

"The man who chases two rabbits, catches neither." [99]
- Confucius

---

99 Source: Confucius. Confucius Quotes. Goodreads. Retrieved from: https://www.goodreads.com/quotes/8688305-the-man-who-chases-two-rabbits-catche

Imagine this: you begin working on a new contract with a client, but then you see a message in Slack. You reply immediately. An alert shows there's a new email from an investor in your inbox, requesting the monthly updates you forgot to send. You start replying, but your co-founder comes over to ask you about an important decision on your new marketing strategy. You jump from one thing to another. At the end of the day, you go home tired, feeling you had a very busy day.

So-called **'Multitasking'** is a common habit among entrepreneurs. In fact, multitasking is a computer term. It describes *"the concurrent execution of multiple tasks (also known as processes) over a certain period of time."* [100] Humans are incapable of focusing on more than one thing at a time. You are either writing a contract, or talking to your employee. You can't do both simultaneously. Instead, you are switching from one to the other.

The switching comes with a high productivity cost. According to a study[101] from the University of London, **"switching makes us dumber than smoking weed"**. The researchers found that people who were asked to smoke weed and do an IQ test lost on average 5 points, while those who were constantly interrupted with emails and text messages before doing the test lost on average 10 points.

Not only that, but if you start a task but don't complete it and then start a new one, you are losing mental capacity even if you are fully focused on the new task. This phenomenon is called attention residue. Sophie Leroy, associate professor of management at the University of Washington notes that: "If you have **attention residue**, you are basically operating with part of your cognitive resources being busy, and that can have a wide range of impacts – you might not be as efficient in your work, you might not be as good a listener, you may get overwhelmed more easily, you might make errors, or struggle with decisions and your ability to process information." [102]

---

100   Source: Wikipedia. Computer multitasking, 2020. Retrieved from: https://en.wikipedia.org/wiki/Computer_multitasking
101   Source: Sollisch, J. Multitasking makes us a little dumber, ChicagoTribune, 2010.
102   Source: Dore, M. How to reduce "attention residue" in your life, BBC, 2020. Retrieved from: https://www.bbc.com/worklife/article/20200130-the-life-hack-to-reduce-admin-and-carve-out-downtime

How to beat Villain 4, Multitasking:
Do one thing at a time

Tools and ideas

1. Use Time Blocking (the Pomodoro Technique)

The Pomodoro Technique, or time blocking, consists of focusing single-mindedly on one specific task or objective for a limited amount of time, with a short break afterwards. The length can vary: you may focus for 25 minutes with a 5 minute break, or 90 minutes with a 15 minute break. It will not only improve your results, but also help you start building your focus-muscle.

2. Complete a task before you move on to the next one

Look at your tasks for the following day. How can you organize your time so that you finish each task before you move on to the next one?

3. Keep a list of distractions

You're in the middle of writing an important email, when you get a great idea for another project. Open your notebook, write down the idea and get back to what you were doing. Later, you look through the list of ideas and decide what to do with them. This simple practice is a game-changer when learning to sharpen your focus.

Villain 5: Perfectionism

It's great to have high standards and prioritise the quality of your product and service. But there's a difference between aiming to do something great and trying to make it perfect. Many entrepreneurs waste too much time and energy trying to perfect things before they deliver. In our experience working with startups this is especially common among creative types: designers, developers and marketers. They want to create beautiful and flawless products before they're unveiled to the world. The challenge is that the clock is ticking - time is limited. Speed is a lot more important than perfection in a startup. Cristobal stresses that "It's better to make 10 decisions fast (knowing that three may be wrong), but to learn and move forward fast, instead of aiming to make three perfect ones."

If you need to build a landing page, would you rather spend three months tweaking and perfecting it internally, or build a quick, 3-day version, launch it, get feedback and improve it accordingly?

How to beat Villain 5, perfectionism:
Aim for great, not perfect!

In NewEurope, it's hard for people to overcome their perfectionism.

Stoyan recently ran a workshop in the Balkans. A founder of a growing startup told him that she was stressed and didn't know what to do. She always tried to look perfect in front of her employees, trying to show them that she doesn't make mistakes. She believed that this would help motivate everyone else to be perfect too, and perform at their best. During the workshop, she realized that trying to be perfect might not be the best strategy. It creates unrealistic expectations for everyone in the team, blocking people from being creative and achieving results.

Embracing creativity and failure: PicsArt

Hovhannes Avoyan is co-founder & CEO of PicsArt, an online photo & video editor with over 150 million monthly active users. Prior to PicsArt, Hovhannes had four successful startup exits. He sees the ability to experiment freely as key to success: "One of the main elements that made me who I am today is experimentation. I work in a highly creative field, and as such, I bring that same way of working to the table. Creativity means you should be confident in your ability to experiment and be free of criticism for it."

Hovhannes has brought this approach to his startups, making sure that his teams look beyond their first instincts, take risks and try something new. "I believe that it is only by trying different avenues that you can arrive at the best answer," he says. "Over the years, I've worked to create a culture where failure is allowed at first. I encourage colleagues, collaborators, and employees…to take creative freedom to try their hand in fresh, new ways. Of course, when something doesn't work out, we can go back to the drawing board and examine what the root cause of failure is." The idea that failing can be positive runs through this ethos. "Experimentation means that mistakes are ok, and they can instead become learning moments, he stresses."It means that no one has the right answer right off the bat. Brainstorming allows for the most interesting, unexpected ideas to come to the forefront."

Tools and ideas

1. Understand where your perfectionism comes from

We usually develop perfectionism in childhood. Take the time to understand where your need for perfection comes from. What triggers it today?
You might want to consult a professional such as a therapist or a coach to help you spot the patterns and come up with a plan for change.

2. Pick your battles

Some things require more attention and detail, while others don't need as much. If you are offering a cybersecurity product, you'd want to ensure the security is flawless. At the same time, many other aspects can be improved on the go. Take your time to consider which activities require 100% effort and attention to detail and which will be fine with 80%, 70% or even 50%. Let go of the need to make everything perfect. That's just not possible.

3. Find the learnings in your mistakes

Create a culture where experimentation is encouraged and the inevitable mistakes are allowed. Empower your team to do its best and aim for great instead of perfect. If employees take a calculated risk and fail, don't be too quick to criticise them. Help them extract the learnings, get back on their feet quickly and do better next time.

Exercise: The Task Importance Matrix

The Task Importance Matrix can help you stay focused on what matters most. Add all your tasks to the matrix, evaluating **the Impact** from Low to High and the **Difficulty** from Easy to Hard. Plotting this on two axes creates 4 quadrants:

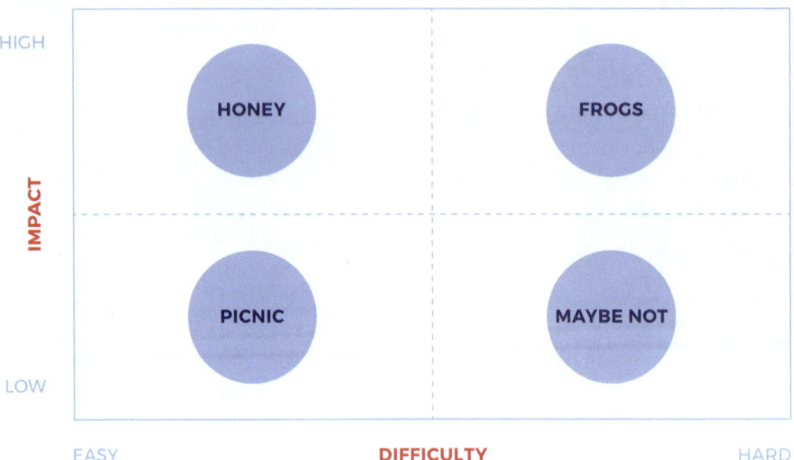

1. Low Impact and Easy (Picnic)

We call this the Picnic because it's like a picnic: easy, fun to do and doesn't take much effort. These are tasks which don't have significant impact.

2. Low Impact and Hard (Maybe Not)

Sometimes we focus on doing things that take a lot of effort, but the expected impact is not helping us progress much towards our goals. This is the **Maybe Not** quadrant.

3. High Impact and Easy (Honey)

These are the tasks that you can confidently take on that also have a high impact on your business. We call them Honey.

4. High Impact and Hard (Frogs)

In the Effective planning chapter, we mentioned the Mark Twain metaphor which Brian Tracy used in his book "Eat That Frog". Your **Frogs** are high impact tasks that are difficult.

Do you spend too much time in **Picnic and Maybe Not** quadrants? What prevents you from 'eating your Frogs'?

KEY TAKEAWAYS

» To thrive as a founder, you need to learn to ignore distractions, take charge and keep your team focused on what matters most.

» **The fewer the priorities, the better the focus.** Your priorities will change as your company evolves.

» **You are probably under-executing. Step up your game!** Create a culture of relentless execution. Inspire your team by example.

» **Start speaking to customers as early as possible.** This mindset will help you focus on what matters to build a better product and grow faster.

» **Beat the 5 villains of Focus & Execution**
1. Combat the **lack of clear priorities by getting clear**. Always know your priorities.
2. Beat the **shiny object syndrome** by **learning to say no**. Stay focused on what you've already started.
3. To address **procrastination**, start **doing**. Understand where your procrastination comes from.
4. Conquer **multitasking** by **doing one thing at a time**. It's a myth that multitasking is productive.
5. Crush **perfectionism** by **aiming for great, not perfect**. Have high standards, but remember: speed is one of your biggest allies.

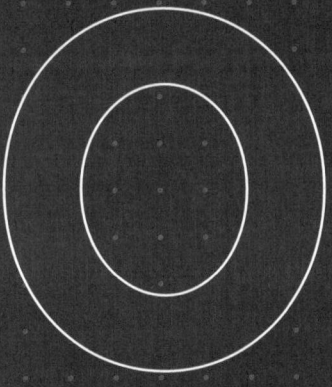

OPTIMAL ENERGY

IN THIS CHAPTER, YOU WILL LEARN:

» The 4 Energy Quadrants
» The ENERGY Framework
  Exercise
  Nutrition
  Excitement
  Relationships
  Good Sleep
  You Time
» The power of building the right habits

"THE HIGHER YOUR ENERGY LEVEL, THE MORE EFFICIENT YOUR BODY. THE MORE EFFICIENT YOUR BODY, THE BETTER YOU FEEL, AND THE MORE YOU WILL USE YOUR TALENT TO PRODUCE OUTSTANDING RESULTS."

- Anthony Robbins[103]

103 Anthony Robbins is an entrepreneur, #1 NY Times best-selling author, philanthropist, life and business strategist. Robbins is the chairman of a holding company comprised of more than 50 privately held businesses with combined sales exceeding $6 billion a year.

Managing your energy

Optimal energy
The state in which you produce and create at your highest level of ability.

Every founder wants their team to perform at its best at all times. Let's have a look at a story of a founder who went too far trying to constantly perform. He was a high-achiever type, working on building his company, putting in long hours with strong commitment. He wanted to succeed. He'd work hard several days in a row, until exhaustion. He'd then take one or two days off to recover. He was passionate about his work. When stress started to pile up, his productive habits started to change, too. He'd exercise less, eat more candy and prioritise work, even when he knew he needed a break.
One day he woke up and couldn't go on. He didn't feel like doing anything. The day became a week, then two weeks. It was obvious that he needed to take a break - and a long one. He couldn't figure out how he'd allowed himself to burn out.
The character of the story was unfortunately me, Stoyan. A few years ago, I went through a serious burnout. It was not a good place to be. My flatmate at the time would make a hot drink and ask me if I wanted one. I couldn't give him an answer. I couldn't decide on anything. I was exhausted. I had to switch off, recover and regroup. It took me nearly two months to get fully back on track.
My experience taught me to be more conscious about how I manage my energy. I realised that I can't perform at my best unless I start paying better attention to myself and my wellbeing. This required me to build a solid foundation, reconnect to my productive habits and make myself a priority again.

If you want to be at the top of your game and maximize your results long term, you need to add **energy** to your list of core priorities. This chapter will explore the habits that will help you and your team master this important area. Though you may find many of the strategies familiar, remember that it's not the knowledge, but the consistency in execution that makes the difference.

"A FOUNDER'S JOB IS TO TAKE GOOD CARE OF THE WELLBEING OF THE TEAM. IN ZEROQODE WE MADE IT A MISSION TO MAKE IT "COOL" TO DISCUSS TOPICS RELATED TO ENERGY AND PERSONAL GROWTH. THAT WAY, PEOPLE STARTED EXCHANGING IDEAS AND INSPIRING EACH OTHER TO GROW. I PERSONALLY ADOPTED A LOT OF DIFFERENT HABITS AND ROUTINES INSPIRED BY THESE OPEN DISCUSSIONS WITH THE TEAM."

- Vlad Larin, co-founder at Zeroqode[104]

---

104   Zeroqode is a Moldovian bootstrapped startup, a platform for no-code web and mobile apps. In 2020 the company employs 40+ employees.

The energy quadrant

To look after yourself and your team, you need to understand your energy and manage it well. Tony Schwartz is the founder and CEO of The Energy Project, a consulting firm that helps individuals and organizations manage their energy more skillfully. He spent years exploring the correlation between energy and performance. One of his tools, **The Energy Quadrant**, explores energy in two dimensions: from low to high and from negative to positive. The optimal quadrant is, of course, the top right corner, the **Performance Zone**, where the energy is high and it comes from a positive place. This is where everyone aspires to be.

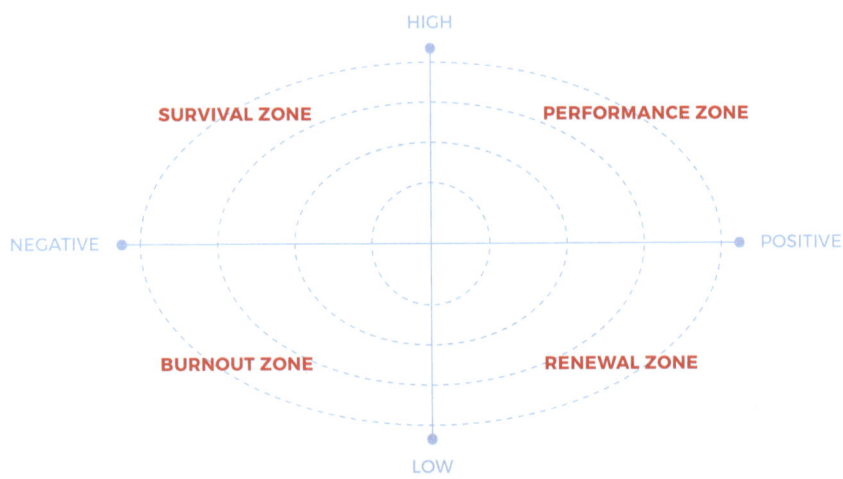

Let's look at the rest of the zones by reflecting on Stoyan's burnout journey. In the early days of building his company, Stoyan would be mainly in the **Performance Zone**. He had positive habits and usually great energy. By constantly trying to be in the performance zone, Stoyan started neglecting his recovery time. This meant that he frequently ended up in the **Survival Zone**, where the energy is high, but negative. For example, Stoyan would work late, not sleep well and wake up tired. Instead of taking the time he needed to recover, he would push through, trying to compensate with caffeine and essentially running on adrenaline. He would skip his workouts and his diet would be less lean. There was plenty of work and it had to get done. After a week or two, Stoyan would end up in the **Burnout Zone** and completely shut down for a day or two, unable to do anything. Then he would recover, only to start the cycle again.

The lifestyle filled with stress and inconsistent rhythm compounded for years, when finally his body couldn't take it anymore. He had to shut down completely and spend several weeks in the Recovery Zone.

We're not made to be sprinting all the time. We perform at our best when we combine high-intensity periods of focused work with proper time for recreation. Think about the Energy Quadrants framework as a reminder. Make sure you find your rhythm between focused-driven time in the Performance Zone and conscious stops in the Recovery Zone.

In simple terms, the best strategy is to be fully focused and engaged when you work and schedule time to unplug completely to recharge afterwards. A study[105] found that without proper detachment, people are unable to fully recover from intense periods of work. Even seemingly harmless activities can be doing more harm than good if they are connected to your job.

The energy framework

Many factors have an effect on your energy. To make it simple, we've developed a model that will help you to stay on track:

---

105 Source: Jonge, J., Shimazu, A., & Dollard, M. Short-Term and Long-Term Effects of Off-Job Activities on Recovery and Sleep: A Two-Wave Panel Study among Health Care Employees, International Journal of Environmental Research and Public Health, 2018.

The ENERGY Framework

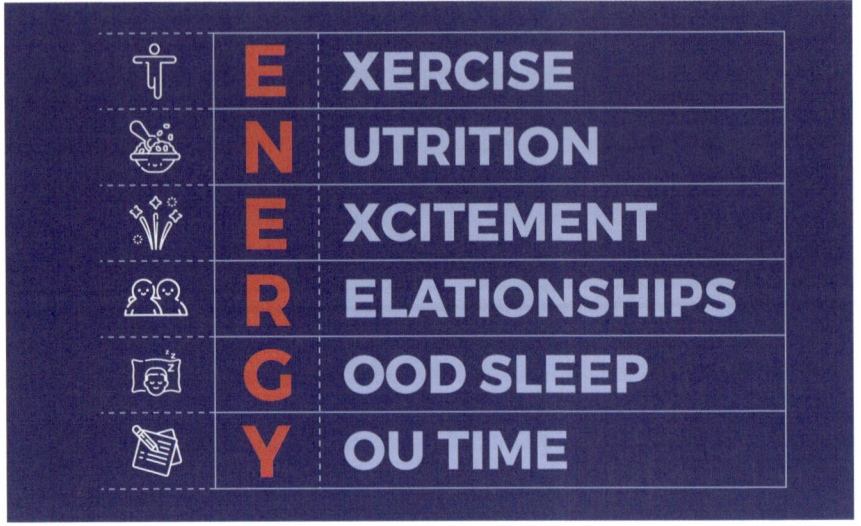

In each of these areas, we'll explore practical strategies and examples.

Exercise

One of the simplest ways to improve your performance is to **exercise** regularly. Exercise provides a number of benefits, including improved concentration, sharper memory, faster learning, prolonged mental stamina, enhanced creativity and lower stress levels[106].

Leeds University conducted research[107] with over 200 employees from different companies with the aim of measuring the effect of at-work exercise on self-reported work performance. On the days the employees exercised, they reported being more productive, managing their time more effectively, having smoother interactions and going home satisfied.

106   Source: Friedman, R., How Exercise Improves Your Performance at Work, Psychology Today, 2014. Retrieved from: https://www.psychologytoday.com/intl/blog/glue/201411/how-exercise-improves-your-performance-work
107   Source: McKenna, J., Exercising at work and self-reported work performance, International Journal of Workplace Health Management, 2008.

As a founder, make exercise your daily priority. Keep it simple, so that you're less likely to skip it. Choose exercise that you enjoy and that fits your lifestyle.

Stoyan used to argue that he didn't have the 90 minutes needed to go to the gym. He'd tell himself he was too busy. In reality, you can always find the time. If you don't have 90 minutes for a full workout, you can still go for a 30-minute run. If you can't prioritise 30 minutes, you can do something in a shorter time.

A great way for a busy entrepreneur to approach exercise is the **Tabata method**. Named after its creator, the Japanese researcher Dr. Izumi Tabata, it lasts only four minutes. It's very simple.

1. **Pick a set of exercises, e.g. pushups, situps, burpees, squats**

2. **Do them for 20 seconds at high intensity followed by a 10-second break, for a total of 4 minutes**

The method is very powerful, can be done at home and according to a study[108] conducted by Dr Tabata, it produces better results than an hour's moderate intensity workout.

"To take care of my energy, I do a lot of sports... If I don't exercise, my mind will take over and f** everything up. I used to do running. These days I like rock climbing, running...I bike to work and I do all my phone meetings walking."
- **Frederikke Schmidt**, founder and CEO of **roccamore**

Whatever type of exercise you choose, find a way to do it regularly. Walking is a simple form of exercise that is proven to be beneficial to the mind. Stoyan hadn't realized the power of walking until he and his partners from Samodiva Masterminds held their quarterly team retreat at the North Wales home of entrepreneur, philanthropist and author Mansukh Patel[109]. Mansukh was very interested in Samodiva's work, offering the team a set of mentoring sessions to help them bring the business to the next level. Before any of these sessions, they would take

---

108   Source: Tabata, I. Effects of moderate-intensity endurance and high-intensity intermittent training on anaerobic capacity and 'VO2max, 1996. Retrieved from:
https://journals.lww.com/acsm-msse/Fulltext/1996/10000/Effects_of_moderate_intensity_endurance_and.18.aspx?sessionEnd=true
109   Mansukh Patel is a scientist, ayurvedic physician, entrepreneur, best-selling author, philanthropist, and peacemaker.

45-60-minute walks in the mountains together. Mansukh is religious about his walking routine. With his busy schedule, running multiple businesses, Mansukh still allocates 2-3 hours each day to walking, including the long walks he takes with his clients or partners.

Walking improves your creativity: Stanford study

According to a report[110] from Stanford University, walking has a positive effect on creative ideation. The researchers carried out four separate studies, all reaching similar conclusions. In one of the studies, **three groups** of people were asked to come up with solutions to a simple creative task. They performed the test in two rounds and the participants were asked to either sit or walk on a treadmill.

Group 1 sat down during both rounds.
Group 2 sat down for round one and walked for round two.
Group 3 walked for round one and then sat down for round two.

Group 1 and Group 2 scored similarly in round one, with an average of 20 creative ideas, while Group 3 did almost twice as well. The only difference was that they were walking.

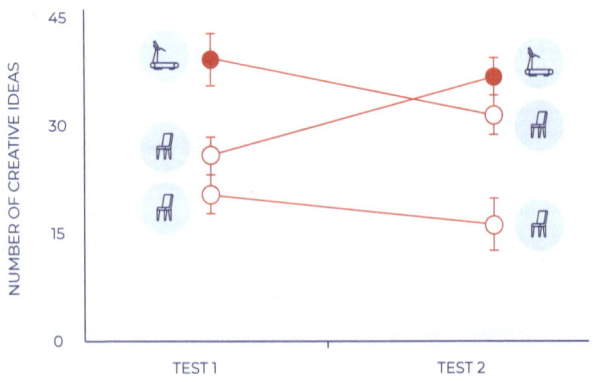

110   Source: Oppezzo, M., & Schwartz, D. L. Give Your Ideas Some Legs: The Positive Effect of Walking on Creative Thinking, Journal of Experimental Psychology: Learning, Memory, and Cognition, 2014.

Interestingly, even though Group 3 sat down during round two after walking in round one, the group's results were still better than the continuously seated Group 1. The walking they had done continued to have a residual effect.

Sometimes you have a problem you can't solve. Go for a walk.

"WE HAVE OUR DAILY CATCH-UP MEETING WITH 3-4 PEOPLE WHILE WE ARE WALKING OUTSIDE THE OFFICE EVERY DAY. IT REALLY WORKS, BECAUSE IT'S STILL A MEETING, SO IT REMAINS SERIOUS AND MANDATORY. NOBODY THINKS THEY ARE EXERCISING. BUT IT'S GREAT EXERCISE. WE WALKED 52KM LAST MONTH."

- Izzet Bogazliyanlioglu, CEO of BoBu[111]

What else can you do to make exercise part of your team culture?

---

[111] Bobu is a Turkish software company helping book and magazine publishers create mobile apps & games for children, without coding.

Nutrition

'You are what you eat!' A good Italian friend likes to joke: "Then I'm pizza or pasta." What you consume has a tremendous impact on your energy and performance. Think about the most productive day you've had lately. What had you eaten that day?

In an article for Harvard Business Review[112], award-winning psychologist and author Ron Friedman, Ph.D., notes that the food we eat affects us more than we realize: *"Just about everything we eat is converted by our body into glucose, which provides the energy our brains need to stay alert. When we're running low on glucose, we have a tough time staying focused and our attention drifts. This explains why it's hard to concentrate on an empty stomach."*

When it comes to food and nutrition, there are numerous recommendations and sources of information. It's a matter of experimentation and understanding what works best for you. We won't go into nutrition in great detail, but only share some general thoughts and guidelines.

When we eat, our bodies break down nutrients into smaller components and absorb them to use as a fuel, a process known as **metabolism**. The main sources of energy are carbohydrates, proteins and fats. Complex carbohydrates (starchy vegetables, whole grain pastas and breads, high fiber cereals) are the most important, because they are digested at a slow and consistent rate. Simple carbohydrates (candy bars, cookies and sweets), however, are absorbed easily and broken down fast. They provide an initial burst of energy, but result in a slump afterwards. Proteins and healthy fats are also very important parts of your diet.

It's your responsibility to choose a regular diet of healthy foods that will fill you with energy. Make unhealthy food choices an exception, rather than a daily habit. When you're hungry, it's easy to choose the faster and cheaper option. It might save you time and a little bit of money and

---

112   Source: Friedman, R., What You Eat Affects Your Productivity, Harvard Business Review, 2014. Friedman is the author of The Best Place to Work: The Art and Science of Creating an Extraordinary Workplace

the budget is usually tight for startup founders. However, making the unhealthy choice usually comes back to bite you[113].

Nutrition and fitness coach Radha Patel shared a simple reminder that can transform your meal times: 'It's not just **what** you eat, but **how** you eat it! Choosing to simply switch off your phone and be present with your colleagues can make a huge change. Even if you can't switch to a better diet right now, bringing more awareness to the way you eat will deliver benefits. Not only do you increase your enjoyment, but you can reduce your caloric intake too, because you're not on autopilot. Even if you're very busy, you can take 15 minutes away from the desk and savour your food, rather than just shovelling it down."

Proper **Hydration** is also important. According to Mitchell et al,[114] the human body consists of up to 60% water. The brain, lungs, heart, liver and kidneys contain between 71% and 84% water, depending on the organ. Even our bones are 31% water. An adult male needs around 3 liters and a female 2.2 liters per day. We get the hydration we need both through the liquids we drink and the food we consume. However, for simplicity, many health experts recommend drinking eight glasses of water per day. If you're not getting enough hydration, drinking more water might be the simplest way to improve your performance.

If water is not your thing, try adding fruits and vegetables to add taste. To get into the habit of drinking regularly, buy refillable bottles for yourself and your team. It's a great investment.

Sodas and similar soft drinks (ice tea, energy drinks) contribute to your daily liquid intake, but they also add high levels of sugar and other unhealthy substances. For example, one liter of Coca Cola contains over 106 grams of sugar - three-to-four times the recommended daily sugar intake. Sugar is highly addictive. It is even compared to cocaine, since it triggers the reward center in our brain, causing the release of dopamine. This hormone gives us a pleasurable 'sugar rush' high, but

---

113 Source: Rodriguez, D., A Diet For Better Energy, Everyday Health, 2012. Retrieved from: https://www. everydayhealth.com/diet-nutrition/101/benefits-of-healthy-eating/eating-for-energy.aspx
114 Source: Mitchell, H. H. et al. The Chemical Composition of the Adult Human Body and Its Bearing on the Biochemistry of Growth, Journal of Biological Chemistry, 1945.

with repeat use, we need more to create the same effect. That's not to say 'never eat sugar'. Just be conscious about the nutritional choices you make, because they have a huge impact on you and your energy.

A few ways to help improve your nutritional habits:

1. Take time to get to know yourself:

We're all different. What diet keeps you at your best and fills you with energy? Notice how you feel after a meal - more or less energised? This is a great indicator of how your body is processing the food!

2. Create a diet plan.

There are millions of diets, nutrition plans and recommendations. Choose a system that fits your lifestyle and beliefs. Keep it simple. Having a strategy will help you make better choices. One option is the **Cheat Day Strategy**: Eat healthily and keep it lean for six days per week - then eat whatever you feel like on your cheat day. It's a great strategy, since you know that what you are craving is not forbidden, only postponed. Often you'll still prefer to eat healthily even on your cheat day.

3. Create an environment that supports you

Get in the habit of buying healthy snacks such as fruits or nuts. Don't have unhealthy foods at home or in the office. It's harder to drink sodas and eat cookies if you don't have any to hand. Have a session with your team to brainstorm how you can build better eating habits. If everyone around you is eating well, you're more likely to do so, too.

Excitement

Excitement is another crucial element that can boost your energy, both at work and outside it.

Excitement during work hours

It's easier to be excited when you do things you love. That's why it's so important that we're driven by purpose and focus on doing what we're passionate about.

The Map of Responsibilities exercise from the Roles & responsibilities chapter can help identify the activities you and your team like the most. You can then aim to do more of these. There will often be times when you have to do tasks that don't excite you, however. As a founder, you can explore ways of making those boring tasks more engaging.

Boost productivity with humor:
Andrew Tarvin[115]

Andrew Tarvin is a Humor Engineer, helping companies to boost their productivity with humor.

"I believe that What gets fun, gets done," he says. "If you were to make your own work a little bit more fun, you're probably more likely to do it. If you were to make your meetings a little bit more fun, people are probably more likely to show up to them. If you were to make your emails a little bit more fun, people would be more likely to respond. If you were to make your social media posts a little bit more fun, you'll probably get a little bit of engagement from them.

Humor at the workplace isn't necessarily about being funny. It's not about becoming a stand up comedian, or a joker, or a clown. But it's rather about making the workplace a little bit more fun, a little bit more light, adding a little bit more levity, so that you can be more engaged in the work that you do."

---

115   Andrew Tarvin is a Humor Engineer and an author of Humor that works:
The missing skill for Success & Happiness at work.

"WHAT GETS FUN, GETS DONE"

- Andrew Tarvin, Humor Engineer

As a founder, you want to show up with passion and motivation. If you're not excited and motivated, then why should anybody else be? Morning stand-ups are a great way to begin the day on a high note by sharing some good energy and sparkle with everyone else in the team. If you're enthusiastic as a leader, your team will feel energized, too.

Excitement outside work

Your business is not your life. It's important that you create a passionate life outside work - it will make you more productive when you're working. To explore the reasons for burnout, Eva de Mol, Violet T. Ho and Jeffrey M. Pollack studied 326 entrepreneurs.[116] The researchers distinguish between "harmonious passion" and "obsessive passion." Entrepreneurs with harmonious passion allow themselves to balance their job with other activities in life without experiencing any guilt or conflict, while also being committed to their work. These entrepreneurs reported higher levels of motivation, attention and focus. Conversely, the entrepreneurs with higher "obsessive passion" had a strong urge to work 24/7. They were more likely to report feeling emotionally drained at work. They were often distracted at work, thinking of the important areas of life that they neglected.

Being passionate about building a successful company is not an excuse to neglect other areas of life. Instead, make sure you have a rich and rewarding life outside work, too. Not only will it give you a better balance, but it will also make you more productive.

Creativity days: MailerLite

MailerLite is a Lithianian email marketing platform with over 100+ employees, most of them working remotely. Co-founder and COO **Ilma Nausedaite** explains that the team has set up a concept it calls 'Creativity days'. Each quarter, every employee is granted one full paid day to do something creative. For

---

116   Source: de Mol, E., Ho, V. T. , & Pollack, J. M. Predicting Entrepreneurial Burnout in a Moderated Mediated Model of Job Fit, Journal of Small Business Management, 2018.

example, you can go to a museum or art gallery, paint or do something fun with your kids. The only rule is that you have to post photos and share your experience on the company's Slack channels. Recently, colleagues have done calligraphy and discussed how it increases your attention span, or fuelled a passionate discussion about Planck keyboards.

"Creativity days help us connect us as a team, start interesting discussions and inspire each other to get out of our comfort zone," explains Ilma. "This is how we widen our point of view and get stories about our team that we can tell our friends: 'Can you guess what my colleague did on Creative day? He built a mechanical keyboard."

"In order to be creative, you have to create space in your mind," notes Ilma. "And often creativity develops by doing something you've never done before."

What fun things do you like to do? What hobbies and passions do you have outside work?

What can you and your team do together that is not related to the business?

Relationships

"Spending time with my family keeps me centered and always helps me to keep things in perspective. Also, I get some of my best ideas when spending time away from the 'grind'."
- **Anders Thomsen**, CEO of **no-more**

The people you spend your time with have a big impact on you and your energy. Humans are social animals and we easily pick up mindsets and behaviours from those around us.

"You are the average of the 5 people you are surrounded by."[117]
- **Jim Rohn**, personal development guru

---

117 Source: Rohn, J. Jim Rohn Quotes, Goodreads, n.d. Retrieved from: https://www.goodreads.com/quotes/1798-you-are-the-average-of-the-five-people-you-spend

Sociologist and physician Nicholas Christakis studied the effects your network has on you[118]. The results showed that if a friend of yours becomes obese, you are 45% more likely to gain weight over the next two-to-four years. More surprisingly, if a friend of your friend becomes obese, your likelihood of gaining weight increases by around 20%, even if you don't know the person. In a similar study[119], Christakis and James Fowler found that if your friend smokes, you are 61% more likely to be a smoker yourself. If a friend of your friend smokes, you are 29% more likely to smoke. And if a friend of a friend of your friend smokes, the likelihood is 11%.

The impact your circle has on you makes it important to always surround yourself with people who will raise your standards and push you forward. Consider the people around you. Who are they? Do they fill you up with energy or are they draining your energy? Are there some people you might need to start seeing less often? Building your startup will take a lot of energy. You can't afford to waste any of it with toxic relationships. If you instead surround yourself with ambitious, positive and driven people, they will help fill up your energy, expand your horizons and provide you with the extra bits of motivation and support needed to succeed.

"HAVING FRIENDS AND STRONG RELATIONSHIPS WITH PEOPLE WHO SUPPORT YOU IS REALLY IMPORTANT. WITHOUT THEM, THE LOWS CAN BE REALLY

---

118   Source: Christakis, N. A. The Spread of Obesity in a Large Social Network Over 32 Years, The New England Journal of Medicine, 2007.
119   Source: Christakis, N. A., & Fowler, J. H. The Collective Dynamics of Smoking in a Large Social Network, The New England Journal of Medicine, 2008.

HARD. HOWEVER, YOU SHOULD ACCEPT THAT MOST NON-ENTREPRENEURS WILL HAVE A HARD TIME RELATING TO YOU. TRY TO HAVE SOME FELLOW ENTREPRENEUR FRIENDS. IT REALLY HELPS."

*- **Boris Borisov**, a co-founder & CPO of **RemoteMore***

Good Sleep

Good quality sleep is crucial. It can be the biggest game-changer when it comes to your energy and ability to perform. Most people need between seven and nine hours of sleep each night. Only a small percentage of people are at their best when they've slept less than seven hours.

However, we don't sleep nearly enough. A recent study by Inc., surveying 500 CEOs, found that more than half of them sleep less than six hours per night. That's a huge problem.

Sleep deprivation impacts your thinking and problem-solving skills. An interesting study[120] found that sleep deprivation has a similar effect to alcohol on your performance. No wonder that, in the US alone, more than 100,000 car crashes yearly are caused by fatigue.

---

120   Source: Alhola, P., & Polo-Kantola, P. Sleep deprivation: Impact on cognitive performance, Neuropsychiatric Disease and Treatment, 2007.

THREE SHEETS TO THE WIND
Research shows the effect on performance of even a moderate level of fatigue is equivalent to or greater than what is considered acceptable for alcohol intoxication.

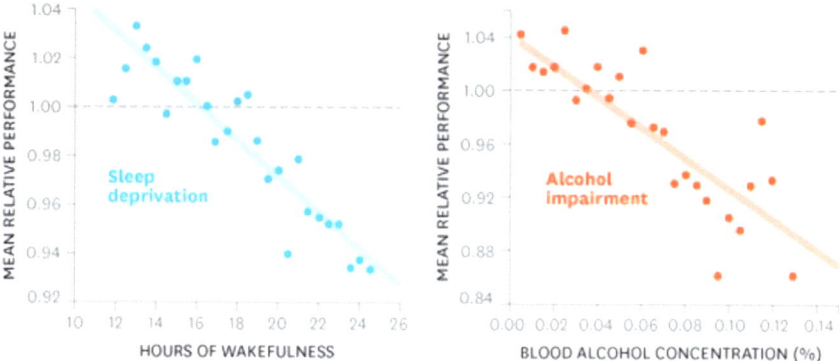

SOURCE DREW DAWSON AND KATHRYN REID'S "FATIGUE, ALCOHOL, AND PERFORMANCE IMPAIRMENT," *NATURE* VOL. 388, JULY 1997.

HBR.ORG

Sleep is more than just rest for our brains. According to an article[121] from the National Sleep Foundation: *"Sleep is an active period in which a lot of important processing, restoration, and strengthening occurs. [...] Our bodies all require long periods of sleep in order to restore and rejuvenate, to grow muscle, repair tissue, and synthesize hormones."*

If you're not well rested, you're robbing productivity from your startup. Lack of good quality sleep is also connected to negative moods, inability to concentrate and inability to do complex thinking, as well as a number of health issues. Prioritising your sleep might be the best investment you make in order to improve your performance.

5 tips to improve your sleep quality:

1. Know yourself and your sleeping rhythm

In his book When: The Scientific Secrets of Perfect Timing author Daniel Pink identifies three types of people, depending on their chronotype[122]:

---

121   ource: The National Sleep Foundation, Why Do We Need Sleep?, SleepFoundation.org, 2020
122   Chronotype = propensity to sleep during a specific time. Source: Pink, D. When: The Scientific Secrets of Perfect Timing, Riverhead Books, 2018.

- **Larks** operate best when they go to bed early and wake up early

- **Night Owls** operate best when they go to bed late and wake up late

- **Third Birds** are somewhere in the middle.

Understanding your own natural rhythm will help you decide when it suits you to go to bed and when to wake up.

2. Decrease screen time before bed

The majority of founders in our workshops admit that the very last thing they do before bed is to check their phones. That's not a good idea, because the blue light from a screen can trick your brain into thinking that it's time to wake up. It can reduce production of hormones, such as melatonin, which help you relax and fall asleep.
Make a habit of turning off all digital devices at least 30 minutes before going to bed. While there are apps that can decrease the blue light, your best bet is to switch off your phone completely and prepare your body and mind for bed.

3. Minimize caffeine intake

What is a startup without massive amounts of caffeinated drinks? Caffeine can have a negative effect on your sleep, however. It has a half-life of about 5 hours, which means that after that time, only 50% of it is out of your system. A study[123] found that consuming coffee 6 hours before bed can decrease the amount of time you sleep by an hour and disturb sleep quality. As a rule of thumb, avoid coffee and other caffeinated products after 2pm and reduce the amount of caffeine you consume.

4. Schedule more time outside

Getting more sunlight during the day has a positive effect on your sleep. Make sure you plan activities that get you out of the office. Combined

---

123   Source: Drake, C., et al. Caffeine Effects on Sleep Taken 0, 3, or 6 Hours before Going to Bed, Journal of Clinical Sleep Medicine, 2013.

with the positive effect of walking or exercise, it can help you sleep better. Remember that exercising too late in the evening can harm your sleep, however. Your body needs time to settle into relaxation before you go to bed.

5. Optimize your bedroom environment

Take good care of the place you sleep in. Change your sheets regularly, air the room before bed and make it nice and cozy. Stoyan oftens uses earplugs and carries a sleep mask when travelling, to make sure his sleep doesn't get disturbed by light or noise.

You time

You time is the time you spend with yourself. Everyone needs their own space once in a while.

Most founders are always busy, jumping from one meeting to another. With additional responsibilities outside work, it can become a habit to put yourself last on the to-do list. Instead, make yourself a priority.

'You time' is your time for **self-care, reflection** and **personal growth**. It's your time to be alone and let your mind digest what has happened. Maybe for you that's your time to walk the dog, or write a journal. Maybe you like meditation or yoga, or perhaps you're an avid reader.

Whatever routine you choose, schedule time in your calendar to be alone, rejuvenate and expand your perspective.

A strong start to the day

One of the best things you can do is to begin your day without checking your phone. Leave it alone for the first hour, instead focusing on getting your mind ready for a successful day ahead. Author Tim Ferriss interviewed over 140 of the world's most successful people for his book Tribe of Mentors. He noted that around 90% of them had a morning meditation or mindfulness practice[124]. This is not an accident. Most of the founders we interviewed for this book also have a **morning routine** to help them give a strong start to the day.

---

124   Source: Ferriss, T. Tribe of Mentors: Short Life Advice from the Best in the World. Ebury Publishing, 2017.

Basics first: Zeroqode

Vlad Larin, co-founder Zeroqode, states that his morning routine is a game-changer, helping him perform at his best. A couple of years ago, inspired by the book Miracle Morning by Hal Elrond, he and his co-founder decided to make their morning routine a major priority. "The idea of the book is that a great way to structure your day is to wake up in the morning and start the day with things that are paramount to your wellbeing, success and goals in life", he explains, "and then you can go about your day. So regardless of what happens you've already taken care of the basics and the important habits: meditating, visualizing, exercising, thinking, planning."

How do you start your morning? What morning routine can you develop?

The power of habits

Adopting all aspects of **The ENERGY framework** can seem easier said than done. To succeed and achieve sustainable results, you need to turn them into habits.

"We are what we repeatedly do. Excellence then is not an act, but a habit."[125]
- Will Durant, an American writer, historian, and philosopher.

---

125   Source: Durant, W. The Story of Philosophy, Simon and Schuster, 1961.

Kicking the caffeine habit: Rune Johansen from no-more

Rune Johansen is a partner and CMO at no-more, the on-demand PowerPoint assistance outfit you met in the Effective Planning chapter. Stoyan coached the team in its early stages. Back then, Rune used to drink five to six cups of coffee each day. He knew it was too much. It'd make him feel groggy in the late afternoon and affect his sleep. He decided to cut down to a maximum of two cups daily. To make the habit stick, Stoyan recommended that Rune set himself a sanction as a way of holding himself to account if he broke the habit. Rune committed to taking the whole team of nearly 20 people to a fancy lunch at his own expense every time he had more than two cups in a day. Six months later, he hasn't broken his new habit once. He has used the same strategy to build several other constructive habits.

Habits are important in everything you do. A study from Duke University[126] found that **more than 40% of our actions are not driven by our decisions, but our habits**. Habits are your mind's way to automate your actions and consequently save energy for more important things. In his book **The Power of Habit, Charles Duhigg** explores this phenomenon: "When a habit emerges, the brain stops fully participating in decision making. It stops working so hard, or diverts focus to other tasks. So unless you deliberately fight a habit, unless you find new routines, the pattern will unfold automatically."[127]

Duhigg helps us understand habits better by introducing The Habit Loop. It has three components: **cue, routine** and **reward.**

---

126   Source: Neal, D. T., & Quinn, J. M. Habits - A Repeat Performance, Association for Psychological Science, 2006.
127   Source: Duhigg, C. The Power of Habit, Random House, 2012.

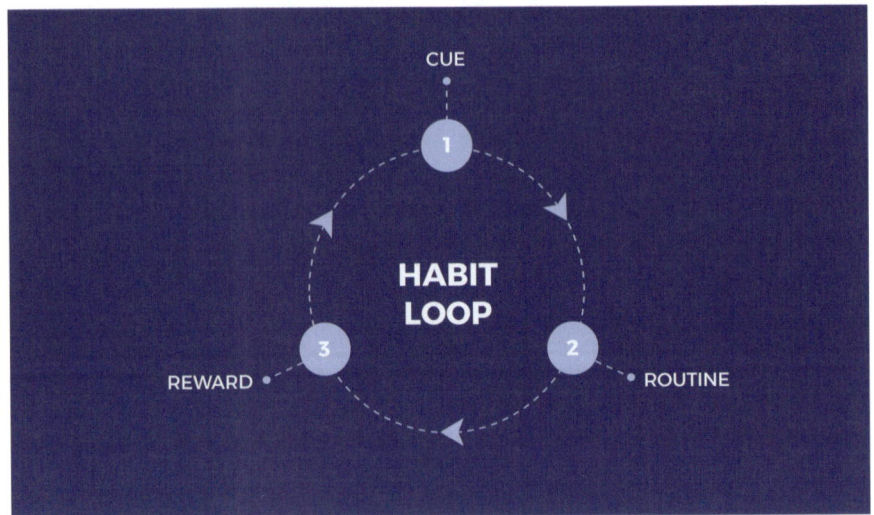

The Cue can be anything that triggers a specific habit: a certain location, time of the day, emotional state and so on. For example, hearing the sound of a coffee machine can be a cue for you to make yet another cup.

The Routine is what you do based on this trigger: the behaviour. In the coffee machine example, you'd make yourself a cup of coffee.

The Reward provides positive reinforcement of the behaviour. This increases the probability you will behave in a similar way in the future. Once you sip from the freshly made coffee, the taste and effect gives you pleasure.

Understanding the Habit Loop can help you spot destructive habits and replace them with constructive ones. Typically, the best way is to **replace the routine**, so that you achieve a similar reward in a more constructive way.

The compound effect

Your habits are the software which helps you to make better choices.

If you get in the habit of consistently making the right choices, this will make a difference when compounded over time. Making the right major choices is of course important, but we shouldn't neglect the importance of seemingly small choices. You may choose to make two extra customer calls rather than leaving for the day, or to have the hard conversation with your co-founder to apologize for reacting inappropriately. You might choose to work out even when you're feeling exhausted after a long day in the office.

The problem is that you often don't see the result of these choices immediately. After all, how much will two extra calls change your revenue today? Probably not much. But what if you make two extra calls every day? In a year of 250-260 working days, that's more than 500 extra calls, which will directly improve your bottom line.

You'll also build momentum. It's likely that you'll become sharper at pitching by practicing and getting feedback, which will improve your conversion rate. Some of the new customers might start referring their contacts to your business. Others, who don't buy immediately, might keep you in mind and come back later, or share your details with a friend. Opportunities will present themselves. This is how your growth becomes exponential rather than linear.

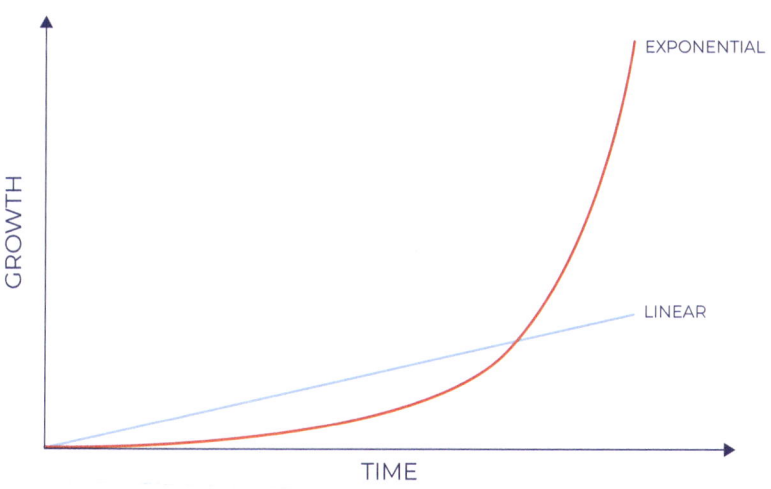

While you can now easily imagine the benefits of choosing to make those calls instead of going for a drink, it can be difficult at the spur of the moment. As humans, we are hardwired to want things immediately: we have an urge for instant gratification.

One helpful strategy is to stop before you make a choice and ask yourself: Is this decision supporting my rational decision-maker or my instant gratification monkey? In other words, how will the outcome of the choice compound over time? Is that in line with the future I'm interested in creating?

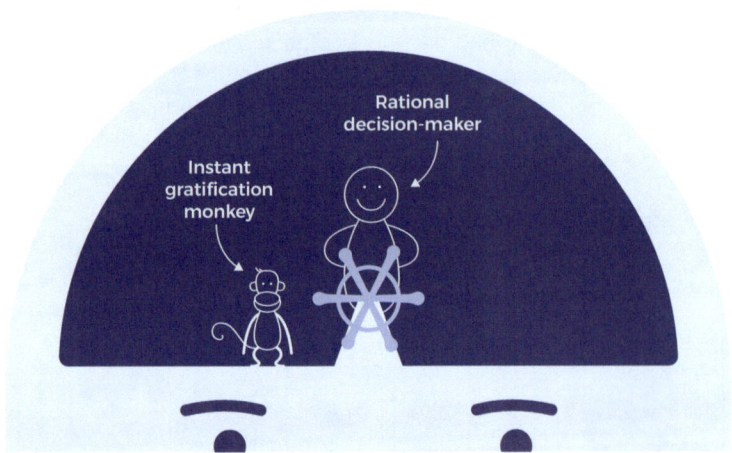

Building your optimal energy team habits

Sustaining and managing your energy is extremely important for every startup founder. Developing the right habits will not only help you improve your performance, but also set the right example, giving your team a role model to live up to. It will improve productivity and wellbeing in the team. Sustaining good habits can sometimes be difficult, but doing so will provide a high return on investment.

Exercise 1: Measure each area of The Energy Framework

This exercise will help you become aware of whether you need to address any of the areas that impact your energy levels.

Step1: Score how well you have been doing in each area of the ENERGY framework during the past week or month.
Step 2: Define concrete actions to help you improve the areas that need immediate attention.

You can also do this exercise as a team discussion.

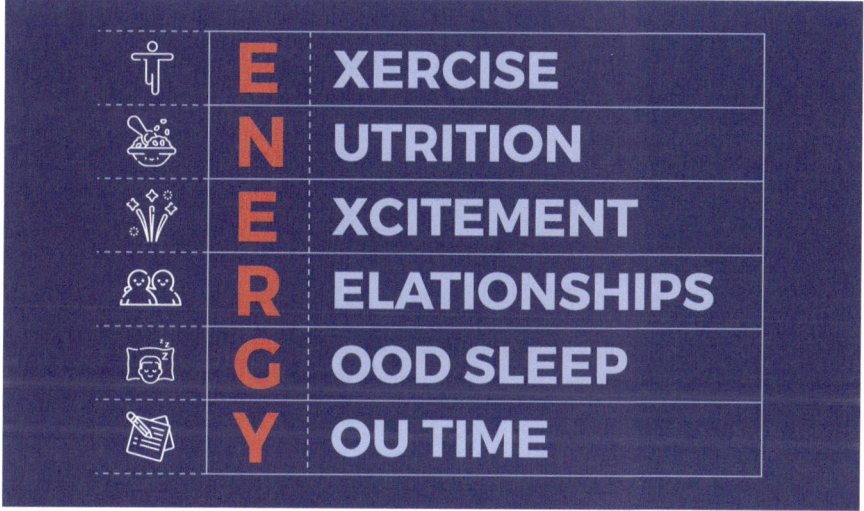

Exercise 2: Managing your energy

How could you plan your day to be more productive?
Each person is unique and it's important to understand your own rhythm. This tool will help you design your days to take advantage of the optimal time for you to do different types of tasks. For example, if you are at your most productive doing creative tasks in the morning when you are rested and alert, you can schedule your meetings for the early afternoon.

Step 1:

Each person in the group individually answers the following question: On a perfect day, which hours of the day would you do tasks in each of these areas?

Creative: Everything that requires creativity. It can be brainstorming, copywriting, designing.
Analytical: Anything that requires logical and rational problem solving.
Administrative: Filing, accounting, paperwork and all types of routine tasks.
Meetings & calls: Everything that requires meeting other people in person, on the phone, or on an online video call.
Strategic thinking: Strategic thinking, reflections, looking at the full picture.
Recreational: Whatever refills your energy. Breaks, sleep, rest and exercise.

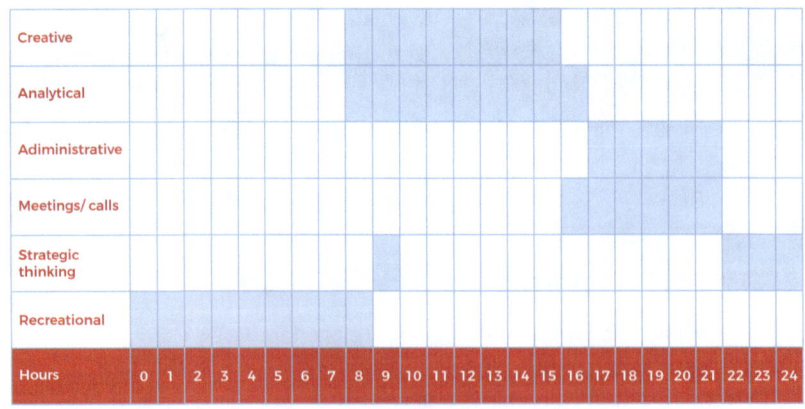

TIME OF THE DAY

Step2:

Share the results with your team and discuss whether there is a need to make any changes in the way each person structures their workload. Mapping your day using this tool will give you the birds-eye view that helps you plan your days effectively and better manage your energy.

KEY TAKEAWAYS

» Team wellbeing has a direct impact on productivity. Create a culture with optimal energy habits. Start by mastering your own habits and lead by example.

» Your body and mind needs recovery. Sacrificing it leads to burnout.

» To keep your energy optimal, become a master of the **6 areas of the ENERGY framework.**

- **E**xercise: Find a daily practice that fits your lifestyle and encourage team activities that include movement.

- **N**utrition: Be mindful of what you eat. Decrease the amount of processed foods, fast foods and sugar. Drink 2-3 liters of water daily rather than soda.

- **E**xcitement: As Andrew Tarvin says: **"What gets fun, gets done"**. Make your workday fun and exciting to help your team perform at their best.

- **R**elationships: Your peer group has a huge impact on your life. Surround yourself with ambitious, like-minded people - you'll need their support during the tough startup journey.

- **G**ood sleep: Good quality sleep can be a major energy game-changer. Improve yours by understanding your sleep rhythm, decreasing screen time before bed, reducing caffeine, getting outside and optimizing your bedroom environment.

- **Y**ou time: In the busy schedule of a founder, it can be difficult to find time for yourself. Create time for self care, reflection and personal growth.

» **Constructive habits are hard to build and easy to destroy.** Understanding the habit loop can help you replace destructive habits with their constructive counterparts.

» **Small choices have the power to make a big difference over time.** Every time you make a choice, remember that it has the power to compound over time.

ROBUST COMMUNICATION

IN THIS CHAPTER, YOU WILL LEARN ABOUT:

» The definition of communication and robust communication
» The four elements of robust communication
» The four areas where constant communication is vital
» The need for a leader to find balance in their communication
» What feedback is and why it is important for startup success
» The key tips on how to provide and receive meaningful feedback
» The value of 360-degree feedback processes
» Seven pitfalls to avoid when building an action plan based on feedback

"AS A COACH, YOU HAVE TO SAY THE RIGHT THINGS TO BRING CONFIDENCE"

- Patrick Mouratoglou, Tennis Coach[128]

---

128   Patrick Mouratoglou is a French tennis coach and sports commentator. He is famous for being the coach of Serena Williams since June 2012. He has coached more than 40 players ranked in top 100 best tennis players in the world.

Why communication matters

Communication
A two-way process of reaching mutual understanding, in which participants not only exchange (encode-decode) information, news, ideas, and feelings but also create and share meaning.

Robust
Strong and unlikely to break or fail.[129]

In this chapter, **robust communication**[130] equals communication that is excellent, authentic and pervasive.

In this chapter, we explain why robust communication is crucially important for a startup and why feedback is one of the main tools for success. This is true as much for an individual as for an organization. We'll focus on the internal communication with and within your team, e.g.:
- Leaders formally speaking **to the team** - founders aligning on the internal communications message, speaking as one to the team, giving direction on priorities and motivating the team; or to an individual - development chats or **giving feedback**
- Leaders formally **listening and receiving feedback from the team**: This involves being open to receiving feedback and having a culture where people feel safe to give feedback to the leaders
- Informal conversations between leaders and teams or individuals: Speaking and listening. This helps the team understand the leaders' point of view and, conversely, enables leaders to better understand teams and individuals.

---

129   Source: Online Cambridge English Dictionary, 2020.
130   Our definition draws on the thinking of Nassim Nicholas Taleb, but is closer to what he termed 'antifragile': Antifragility is beyond resilience or robustness. The resilient (robust) resists shocks and stays the same; the antifragile gets better.

We've already touched on the subject of communication. It's not surprising that it crops up repeatedly: When working with a team, you always need to communicate.

In the post-Soviet culture of NewEurope, silence is common. This lack of communication can bring down a startup. A problem can often be solved in seconds if those responsible are aware of it. If a company has a culture of openness, responsibility and honesty rather than silence, problems don't escalate to become disasters.

If talent, innovation and extreme customer focus are the main drivers of success for your company, a fundamental part of making sure your organization runs well is superb communication across all parts of the organization and to all stakeholders. Build your company on an unshakeable foundation of robust communication.

Fundamentals of robust communication

Communication is not a one-way process. It should connect all individuals working at different levels of the company. Communication can and should be constant, creative and meaningful. A leader who is bad at communicating with other people will, sooner or later, cause misalignment and misunderstanding in the organization.

Communication is a huge challenge for CEOs because they are time-poor. It's not unusual that they choose to save time by cutting back their personal involvement in the overall internal company communication. They spend less time talking and listening to their own team. This is a huge mistake. A study[131] surveying some of the top corporate CEOs in the US found that 25% of their time was dedicated to people and relationship building (with an additional 16% focused on organization and culture). While each business is different, this gives us a good indication that at least one fourth of a leader's time should be dedicated to communication.

---

131   Source: Porter, M., Nohria, N. How CEOs Manage Time, Harvard Business Review, 2018.
Retrieved from: https://hbr.org/2018/07/the-leaders-calendar

"AFTER GROWING PAST 10 PEOPLE, PEOPLE GET LEFT OUT OF THE NORMAL "HALLWAY" CONVERSATION AND WANT A FORMAL PROCESS TO ENSURE EVERYONE KNOWS COMMON EXPECTATIONS."

*- **Tim Hall**, co-founder and CEO, **Simporter**, a leading FCMG analytics startup*

Moreover, communication will only get more difficult as your company, team and circle of potential investors grow. It's therefore important to develop the right communication habits at the very beginning.

"When I stopped doing 1-1s with the team - then our culture started to suffer. As soon as I realized it, I started prioritizing them again, and the team and our culture got back on their feet."
- ***Konstantin Djelebov***, Co-Founder and CEO of ***phyre***, a Bulgarian e-wallet startup.

Even if you're not a leader, you need to understand the importance of communication. If you're a leader, act like a sports coach. Consider how a coach communicates with the players during a time-out and the effect it has on the team spirit and the results. For those of you not familiar with sports coaching, we recommend watching Coach Phil Jackson in action with top NBA basketball team Chicago Bulls in the documentary **The last dance** on Netflix. It depicts very well how coaching helps improve team spirit and communication.

So, be that coach, motivate your team! Bring your positive energy to the table every time someone fails. Find a golden ratio[132] between communicating the positive and the negative. Do it in a manner that creates more energy and willingness to move forward.

The four elements of robust communication

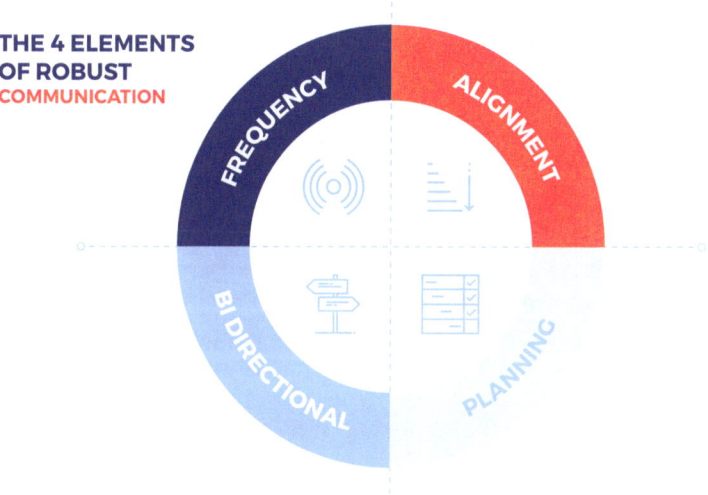

THE 4 ELEMENTS OF ROBUST COMMUNICATION

Four main elements form the core of effective, robust communication: **Frequency** relates to how often you communicate with other team members. Be consistent: If you don't speak to your entire team at least once a week, the company will quickly start disengaging. In a 2019 study[133], Marcus Buckingham and Ashley Goodall found that while team

---

132   Term widely used during the Renaissance in the art scene, but refers originally to a mathematical term. More information: https://en.wikipedia.org/wiki/Golden ratio
133   Source: Buckingham, M., Goodall, A NINE LIES ABOUT WORK: A Freethinking Leader's Guide to the Real World, Harvard Business Review Press, 2019.

leaders who check in once a week on average see a 13 percent increase in team engagement, those who check in only once a month see a 5 percent decrease in engagement. Check in with your team no less than once a week.

Alignment between co-founders is essential. You may have come across children who play their parents off against each other by asking favours from the one most likely to say yes. This kind of game can't be allowed to happen in a startup. The co-founders have to be completely aligned on any message that goes out. They may have different styles of communicating, but the message has to be the same. Everyone should be driven by the same vision, objectives and reasons.

Communication must be **bi-directional** - everyone both speaks and listens. As a leader, you need to establish communication channels between all levels and teams across the company in order to create a culture of open communication. Only when everyone can both speak and listen openly, you'll have a culture that fuels success and commitment.

Planning and scheduling time for your communication is vital. Let's imagine that you'd like to be the leader who writes interesting, useful and motivating emails to the whole team. You do this on Fridays every two weeks. The writing takes time, though, and as your agenda fills up, you drop it. This is a mistake. Everything in a startup has to be planned and communication is no exception. Put it in your agenda at a time when you know your mind is fresh. Don't delegate this task. Your team wants to hear from you, not from your communications- or HR team. They don't want a politically correct message; they want to know what's on your mind.

As an example, here is how Cristobal as CEO of Startup Wise Guys, together with his COO has built a robust communication set-up. At the time of writing, SWG has a team of 35 people working in more than five different locations.

Type of meeting	Frequency	Covering
Operations update	Weekly	Update call: CEO and COO update the full team on company status and the main deliverables for the week.
Check In	Weekly	Each manager has one-to-one 15 min Monday calls with direct reports, covering weekly priorities and how they can help.
Monthly one-to-one	Monthly	Each manager meets each of their direct reports. Review of priorities, achievements, challenges and giving and receiving feedback. Strategy update
Strategy update	Monthly	For all employees. The CEO summarizes financial and operational results and the status of the main battles (yearly and quarterly strategic priorities). Typically a five-hour call with several breaks.
Managers call	Monthly	Run by the COO. All managers reporting to the CEO openly share their challenges. The CEO and COO listen, provide feedback and, where needed, initiate projects to address any issues.

Type of meeting	Frequency	Covering
Operations update	Weekly	Update call: CEO and COO update the full team on company status and the main deliverables for the week.
Check In	Weekly	Each manager has one-to-one 15 min Monday calls with direct reports, covering weekly priorities and how they can help.
Team offsite (ideally in person, but we have run these online when the Covid-19 crisis caused travel restrictions)	Quarterly	Unlike the strategy updates, the quarterly offsites are as interactive as possible to help management collect feedback and ideas, engage the team and emphasize accountability and ownership.
Strategy Session	Twice a year	Twice a year, the quarterly team offsites expand to become strategy sessions, which also involve team building activities. These sessions are focused not only on strategy but also on strengthening the company culture.

Four areas to communicate about constantly

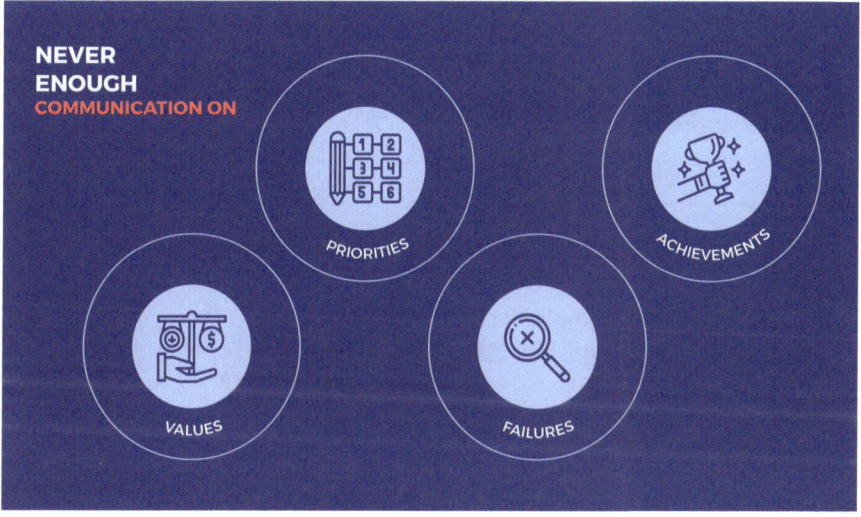

A startup can never have enough internal communication. No doubts or problems should be hidden away in silence. However, we have identified four areas where constant communication is particularly important.

1. Values: In the Purpose & Values chapter, we explained the concept of values in-depth. It is fundamental to keep talking about them constantly. Include your values in every company narrative when talking to your team, employees or external stakeholders. Why is visibility and repetition so important? Remember that most companies that are scaling are growing their people as aggressively as their results. If you double your headcount every year, many of your employees are hearing about your values for the first time.

2. Priorities: You need to constantly remind people of their priorities, day after day. If you don't they may think that yesterday's priority is no longer one today. They may focus on something else. Even if you feel that you have clearly explained the priorities, some people may not have grasped them. If this happens, keep reiterating the message in a friendly manner.

3. Achievements: Any startup will have setbacks. To counteract the inevitable daily problems, start celebrating every tiny victory. Every email that brings positive feedback, every job well done, every new customer and all the other **achievements** along the way. If you only talk about failures and problems, you will create a negative atmosphere. So, if something good happens – celebrate! Put it on Instagram. Bring a cake to the office. Write a nice email. Shout it out loud.

Positive Feedback Meetings: roccamore

Frederikke Schmidt, Founder & Creative Director at roccamore, a Danish high-end shoe brand that aims to create comfortable high heels for cool and confident women, has monthly feedback meetings where each team member takes turns to talk. There's one important caveat: They're only allowed to emphasize achievements and speak positively about their colleagues.

---

4. Failures: When a mistake is made, it is equally important to be open about it. Admit that you've f****d up, whatever the reason was. If you start hiding your mistakes, you lose an important opportunity to learn and improve. Failure is the foundation of success. In The last dance, NBA superstar Michael Jordan mentions how losing in the playoffs just after he came back from retirement was key to refocusing the Chicago Bulls' team. The season was over. They couldn't change what had happened, but over the next summer they trained like never before and came back stronger. The following season, they won their sixth championship ring. If you hide and don't talk about your feelings, mistakes and what you learned from them, nothing will change. Instead, learn from your failures and practice even harder. We've lost, we move on, and we'll win next time!

The value of being honest about failure:
SessionStack

SessionStack empowers support teams, enabling them to create the best support journey experience for their customers. The company was founded in Bulgaria, but today more than half of its customers are US-based. SessionStack has seen phenomenal growth over the past two years.

Alexander Zlatkov, co-founder and CEO, learned the hard way how important it is to talk about difficulties with the team. When the company first started out, management communicated mostly about any situation's potential positive impact on the business. He believes that this is typical for first-time founders, emanating from excitement and even naivety. Soon enough, they realized that creating this protective ring around the team was very dangerous, as it meant teams would be surprised when something hit the company hard. "Sometimes difficult choices have to be made," Alexander notes. "If the team understands clearly that short-term painful decisions will lead to long-term benefits for the organization, it will make them resilient and more connected with the global company vision and direction."

By shielding the team from the difficulties, you're not leveraging their full potential: They have input that could help. The SessionStack executive team evolved its communication style. The managers started explaining both the potential benefits and downsides of any situation. It has helped develop a strong team that is better able to cope with the tough reality.

The leader: How to balance communications

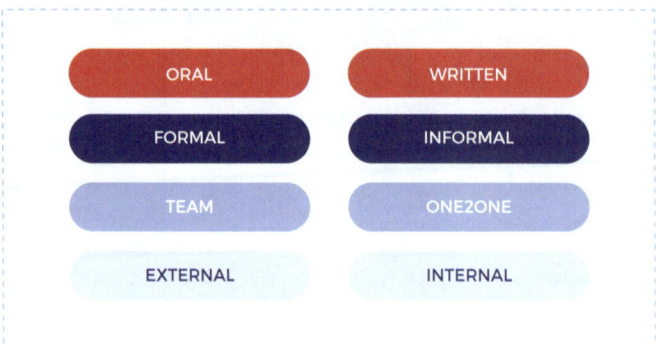

**COMMUNICATION STYLE:
"THE RIGHT BALANCE"**

ORAL	WRITTEN
FORMAL	INFORMAL
TEAM	ONE2ONE
EXTERNAL	INTERNAL

"THE ART OF COMMUNICATION IS THE LANGUAGE OF LEADERSHIP."[134]

- James C. Humes, *US author and former US presidential speechwriter*[135]

"[The] Startup industry is a trust business. It's about nothing but trust until IPO and then it's about numbers to satisfy large stock market investors. This means that trust has to be built in all relations and

---

134 Source: Humes, J. Quote. Rock Solid Business Development, n.d. Retrieved from: https://rocksolidbizdevelopment.com/ourblog/the-art-of-communication-is-the-language-of-leadership/
135 Along with William Safire and Pat Buchanan, James C. Humes is credited for authoring the text on the Apollo 11 lunar plaque. He was a speechwriter for 5 US presidents.

communication. It goes vertically up and down and horizontally among team leads. The CEO is the main manager of the relationships between shareholders, board, management, team leads and the team. I don't see any opportunity for the CEO to be someone he or she is not as a person. So, my lesson learnt from day 1 is to be who you actually are and to communicate the way you do. Obviously, honesty, respect and balance are the key words and shouting at people is absolutely no-go",
- **Kaidi Ruusalepp**, Founder & CEO of **Funderbeam,** one of the leading European Crowdfunding and trading platforms for private companies, with headquarters in Estonia and investors from 128 countries

A CEO is often seen as the **'Chief Motivation Officer'**. Not every leader is an optimist by nature. As Kaidi points out, above all, you need to be your real self. But you have to find a way to motivate your team. Even when you feel down, you have to drive the team forward. All eyes are on you: if you stop believing, your team will stop believing.

As the lead communicator in your company, you need to balance communications to work well for your team. Consider the way you talk to the team, the things you say and the means you choose to share important information. Make sure each team member gets a share of your attention. The trick is to know what your team needs at any given moment, so you can adapt what to say and how you say it to drive the team and business forward. As a leader, this means you must spend time listening to understand what your team needs.

By creating a habit of informal gatherings with your team, such as dinners or Friday breakfasts, you put in place unique listening opportunities for yourself as a leader. You might discuss the company or its results, talk about how the team feels or get feedback from your team.

Complement team gatherings with one-to-one meetings. Inviting an employee to a coffee alone with you may be everything you need to do to make them happy. Just ask them how they feel. By getting your personal attention, this individual will feel you value, trust and care for them. It will also help you understand how your communication with that important employee can be adjusted to be effective.

Your choice of communication channels also needs to be balanced - in particular the amount of oral versus written communication. Our overall rule is that every time you communicate a message in a group setting or one-to-one, you follow up in writing to make sure everyone is on the same page. Conversely, every time you send an important message in writing, make sure you follow up with several team members in person or on the phone to see if the message has been understood correctly. This creates a good balance between oral and written communication.

These days, in particular due to the 2020 Covid crisis, CEOs and leaders have to rely on video calls more than ever. As a company grows, recorded presentations and company calls are common. If you follow up with an engagement survey to collect feedback, make sure you share the results with the team.

"Over time, you become much more mindful about how you communicate and the impact it has on your team. It's easy for a 5 person team to know your ups and downs, what you mean versus what you say. But with a larger company, you cannot assume that all 100 people will know your mood [and] understand your communication style."
- Ashot Tonoyan, Managing Director, **ServiceTitan Armenia**[136]

---

136 ServiceTitan is the world's leading and fastest-growing software technology platform for the trades. It currently has more than 4,000 customers and more than 1000 employees. ServiceTitan is the first Armenian-founded tech unicorn and it has a team of 60+ people in Yerevan.

"AVERAGE PLAYERS WANT TO BE LEFT ALONE.
GOOD PLAYERS WANT TO BE COACHED.
GREAT PLAYERS WANT TO BE TOLD THE TRUTH."

- Doc Rivers, NBA Coach (champion with Boston Celtics in 2007-08)

The importance of feedback for success

"OPERATING WITHOUT FEEDBACK IS LIKE COOKING WITHOUT TASTING THE FOOD"

- Joel Peterson, Chairman of the board, JetBlue Airways

Feedback
A process in which the effect or output of an action is 'returned' (fed back) to modify the next action.

Feedback is like cooking. When you cook something, you ask people to taste it and whether they like it. If you're cooking a new code in a startup, don't keep it to yourself. Ask someone to 'taste' your work and give you feedback to help make it better. As a leader, you need to be good at both giving and receiving feedback. Seek opportunities to do both, both formally and informally. It isn't enough to have semi-annual, formal check-ins. Feedback should be continuous.

A powerful feedback exercise is cited both by INSEAD author **Jennifer Petriglieri** in Couples that work[137] and **Ray Dalio** in his book *Principles*[138].

---

137   Source: Petriglieri, J. Couples That Work: How Dual-Career Couples Can Thrive in Love and Work, Harvard Business Review Press, 2019.
138   Source: Dalio, R. Principles: Life and Work, Simon & Schuster, 2017.

It involves two people giving each other feedback. One person provides their feedback for a set time - 2 or 3 minutes - without being interrupted. The person receiving the feedback listens carefully and summarizes the feedback they've received. Then the tables turn and the other person gets the opportunity to speak.

We believe in helping people perform better by giving them an assessment of how they are doing and the ways in which they can improve. That sometimes means giving praise and sometimes constructive criticism. While we were convinced of the transformative power of feedback, our hunch was always that people generally weren't very keen on hearing the negatives. A great study published in Harvard Business Review, *Your Employees Want the Negative Feedback You Hate to Give*[139] proved us wrong. The study has a good balance of answers from the US and other markets and shows conclusively that people feel constructive criticism is the most helpful form of feedback:

"...people want corrective feedback, even more than praise, if it's provided in a constructive manner. By roughly a three to one margin, they believe it does even more to improve their performance than positive feedback...92% of the respondents agreed with the assertion, "Negative (redirecting) feedback, if delivered appropriately, is effective at improving performance."... People believe constructive criticism is essential to their career development. They want it from their leaders. But their leaders often don't feel comfortable offering it up. From this we conclude that the ability to give corrective feedback constructively is one of the critical keys to leadership, an essential skill to boost your team's performance that could set you apart."
– Jack Zenger and Joseph Folkman, Your Employees Want the Negative Feedback You Hate to Give

If you have team members who don't understand the importance and benefit of feedback, it's your responsibility to coach them to become good at both giving and receiving it. A lack of understanding is never an excuse not to give feedback.

---

139   Source: Zenger, J. (author, speaker and HR/Leadership coach) & Folkman, J. (author, speaker and HR/Leadership coach), Your Employees Want the Negative Feedback You Hate to Give, Harvard Business Review, Jan 15, 2014. Retrieved from: https://hbr.org/2014/01/your-employees-want-the-negative-feedback-you-hate-to-give

How you give feedback also matters. Any team member will be more receptive to negative feedback if it's given constructively, but take the time to make both your negative and positive feedback matter. Constantly saying 'Good Job!' can end up being counter-productive, as employees may find it patronizing. Instead, tell people why they did a good job. It'll take you 20 more seconds, but the person will feel the difference. This can be simple, such as: "J, love the way you used those new graphs to explain our performance. Please share more with the team and keep going." This tiny addition will encourage them to do even better next time.

REGULAR FEEDBACK MAKES
YOUR TEAM HAPPIER

35%
Of employees are
happy at work

After receiving
feedback and
recognition

51%
Of employees are
happy at work

Feedback has multiple benefits. Statistics show that in general, employees want more feedback. The more feedback we give them, the happier they are. In a study[140] conducted by the Estonian strategic objectives tracking and employee engagement company WorkDone, 35% of the employees were happy at work when first surveyed. The share increased to 51% after they received feedback and recognition. Since it's well known that happier employees are more likely to stay

---

140   Source: Kirill. Employee feedback: Why It Matters and How To Use It. Weekdone Leadership Survey, available at: https://blog.weekdone.com/employee-feedback-why-it-matters-and-how-to-use-it/
Weekdone is an Estonian startup founded in 2012 and named top 5 employee engagement software recently.

longer at their jobs, this makes the importance of feedback even clearer.

Failing to seek out and listen to employee feedback can cause significant problems. Imagine that you have spent a long time, perhaps six months, looking for a strategic hire. You're busy, and don't take the time to sit down with them regularly to ask how things are going. After six months, the person quits. They weren't happy. Now let's do the math. You have put in six months of time and effort to find the new hire, but can't find time for a cup of coffee to understand whether you need to improve their day-to-day experience? If we don't allocate the time for feedback, we lose time, money and precious resources. Time invested in feedback sessions is time well spent.

Feedback may limit escalation of issues to the CEO. When you hear two of your direct reports clashing, encourage them to have a mutual feedback session instead of intervening to help them solve it. Over time this not only limits escalation but also makes your team stronger and capable of solving issues that arise as the company grows.

We recommend using tools available in the market to facilitate feedback and employee engagement processes, but don't outsource these activities to external agencies - at least not while your company employs less than 100 people. Instead, show that feedback is important and that management is willing to make time for it.

By using "sandwich" feedback method, people actually don't understand if they did well or not. You need to give them honest feedback. It has to be balanced and motivating, helping the employee understand their strengths, areas of developments and need for improvements as a person and teammate".
- *Kaidi Ruusalepp*, CEO and Founder, *Funderbeam*

How to provide and receive feedback

"To make feedback effective, you need to understand the personality of the person receiving feedback: Some people are very emotional, even though they might be great at what they do. The feedback must be structured in such a way not to make a person feel threatened in any way. Once a person feels threatened in some way, they can get very defensive, and then the discussion will be highly unproductive and most likely won't have the desired outcome. At the end of the day, it's your responsibility to make your team as efficient as possible"
- **Alexander Zlatkov**, co-founder and CEO of **SessionStack**

The seven key tips to help you to provide meaningful feedback

7 KEY TIPS TO HELP YOU PROVIDE MEANINGFUL FEEDBACK

1 UNDERSTAND THE GOAL

2 FOCUS ON THE ISSUE, NOT THE PERSON

3 PUT YOUR MESSAGE IN WRITING AS WELL AS DELIVERING IT VERBALLY

4 GET THE RIGHT BALANCE BETWEEN POSITIVE AND NEGATIVE COMMENTS

5 MAKE IT ONE2ONE

6 PLAN CAREFULLY AND FEEDBACK CONTINUOUSLY

7 CLEAR NEXT STEPS

1. Understand the goal

The purpose of constructive feedback is to encourage the other person to move into a problem-solving conversation with you, not to 'change' for you. The purpose of positive feedback is to help the person more fully own and leverage their strengths.

2. Focus on the issue, not the person

Focus on employees' behaviors (what they do) rather than on their personality traits (what they're like). It's also important to focus on how you felt, rather than pointing fingers and accusing the person of being 'bad'. Negative feedback can seem painful when it's first received.

Language matters when communicating. Avoid characterizations or labels such as 'you're not empathetic'. Don't make up stories about why they acted in a certain way, such as 'you don't give a damn'. Make sure you speak honestly about how you felt, but remember that saying 'I feel that you are not empathetic' and 'I feel that you don't give a damn' is not solving anything.

3. Put your message in writing as well as delivering it verbally

A message in writing can help reduce any initial emotional impact and focus on the facts. It also ensures both parties have understood the feedback on an aligned way (or not, and then there is an opportunity to correct it).

4. Get the right balance between positive and negative comments

It's unpleasant and generally unhelpful to put negative feedback front and center. However, the boss who'll bend over backwards to avoid confrontation by only offering positive words is no more helpful. If you focus only on the negative or positive, you're not creating a deep, balanced relationship with your team members. Provide honest negative feedback when needed, but always do it in a constructive manner.

Cristobal's friend and mentee Goda Juskeviciute, who has recently joined SWG, established her own managerial rule for feedback-giving. When writing down problems, she always adds the same amount of positive things about the person. Depending on whether she is having a 'catch up on performance' or a 'resolve an issue' feedback session, she either starts with the positive or the negative feedback, given in a respectful way. She always keeps a 50/50 balance.

5. Make it one-to-one

Perceived wisdom is that you praise people in public and criticize them in private. However, for some people even praise is better delivered in a private meeting rather than in public. Some people simply don't like being the center of attention.

This can also be the case when you're asking people to contribute after team presentations, something we've found to be a real issue in the Baltics and to certain extent in all of NewEurope. After the CEO gives an important presentation to the team, you ask for questions or feedback and no one speaks up. If someone does, others react in one of two ways: they think the person is showing off or they wonder who they think they are, taking the liberty to challenge a manager. This is problematic, but you have to be aware of it if you are managing teams in this region. Always allow opportunities for face-to-face feedback, as it can make it easier for a person to say what they really think. Once trust is established, the group behaviour can be changed through a culture of transparency and honesty.

6. Plan carefully and feedback continuously

Continuous performance feedback is important. Take time to plan it carefully - don't just put it in your agenda. Have a plan for what you will say, how you will say it and what suggestions you have as next steps. Then ask them to join you for coffee and create a relaxed atmosphere. Wait until after a project is completed or problem resolved. Never give feedback when you are still in the midst of the situation.

7. Clear next steps

A clear and aligned understanding of what comes next for both parties is essential. Providing feedback in writing also allows you to summarize the next steps that you and the employee agree on in the conversation.

Six key tips to help you **be a good receiver** of feedback

6 KEY TIPS TO HELP YOU BE A GOOD RECEIVER OF FEEDBACK

1	2	3
DON'T BE DEFENSIVE	BE CURIOUS. REPEAT. ASK QUESTIONS	SIGNAL UNDERSTANDING

4	5	6
THANK YOU, THANK YOU, THANK YOU	KNOW WHEN TO STOP AND WHEN TO PAUSE	RESPOND PROMPTLY AND BE CONSTRUCTIVE

1. Don't be defensive

Avoid justifying and explaining yourself, or arguing that the other person's feedback and assessment is wrong. Remember that feedback is data and having data is better than not having it. Data expands our choices and results in healthier and more productive relationships.

2. Be curious. Repeat. Ask questions.

Practice telling yourself: 'This person is upset with something I did. If I can figure out what that is, I can move towards solving the problem'. This mindset will allow you to receive and process more data. Practice asking 'why' as a way to keep showing curiosity and collecting data. If they are annoyed with you, accept it and ask them to help you understand why they're feeling that way.

3. Signal understanding

Demonstrate that you listen and understand by paraphrasing and repeating back what you have heard, for example: "I hear that the fact that sometimes I don't respond to your texts for several days is what leaves you feeling that I'm not committed." Building understanding is better than getting into an argument about whether or not you are committed.

4. Thank you, thank you, thank you

Someone who gives you feedback cares enough to say something. You should always thank the giver. This is even more important when you are in an equal or more senior position. In many cases, giving you feedback will have taken them a lot of courage.
5. Know when to stop and when to pause

It is OK, and can even be preferable, to take a break and negotiate a time to return to the conversation. The feedback giver may have waited until he or she was really upset before saying anything - if this happens, it can be easier to give it a bit of time.

6. Respond promptly and be constructive

As a leader, always respond positively, promptly and constructively when you are given feedback. Not doing so is one of the biggest mistakes we see leaders make. If an employee takes the time out of their busy day to give you valuable feedback, you should always give a full response. You don't have to do so immediately, though. If you need time to reflect, acknowledge receipt of the feedback, say thank you and let the person know when you will get back to them. Make sure you can honor the time frame you give and put a reminder in your calendar.

Holistic feedback strategy: Plan to make feedback an integral part of your startup

No matter how small a company is, you need information to flow in all directions and a system to enable this. Information will naturally flow top down but you need to create opportunities and systems for it to flow bottom up. This is not just important for big companies.

On an ongoing basis, aim to measure, manage and act on results across three dimensions:

- **Employee Engagement** - measuring the extent to which employees are motivated, satisfied, and involved in your organization. When doing it for the first time, make sure you define a clear initial objective and which insights you want to focus on or the startup needs focus at this current moment. When doing it on ongoing basis, (re)start by setting up an initial engagement baseline, calibrating with previous ones, going deeper into particular areas (usually those areas weaker on previous surveys) and measure again

- **Employee Experience** - Employee observations and perceptions about their experience. In a startup, define and measure this at least at three key points – recruitment, onboarding and exit

- **Employee Effectiveness** - To improve results, effectiveness is essential. In order to perform effectively, your employees need to know when they are not doing the right thing and how to contribute better. This is usually done through 360-degree methodologies for employees, but also needs to be measured for managers in 180-degree feedback.

In smaller organizations that have to adjust fast to a rapidly changing environment, a combination of regular engagement pulse surveys and weekly one-to-ones that explore both performance and engagement could work well. The management team needs to put this in place early on, with a leader to drive it.

If you want a formal process of collecting and sharing feedback, a 360-degree feedback review can make sense for both startups and scaleups. It's designed to gather feedback about an employee from everyone they work with, giving a team member feedback from all angles. Supervisors, direct reports and peers all share their views on a person's skills, behavior and impact.

For a person to improve or track their feedback, the measurements need to be systematic and comparable. Aim to ensure that questions don't change dramatically over time and that results are weighted as the number of people responding changes.

Regardless of how you collect the information, what matters is how you use it. When developing a path to change based on the insight you have gathered, ensure you:

When developing a path to change based on the insight you have gathered, ensure you:

1	Don't rush into action until you have evaluated the results. Engage the team in this process
2	Avoid getting stuck in analysis paralysis. Turn insights into actionitative assessment
3	Don't take the survey results personally
4	Understand how negative feedback shows opportunities for improvement for you as a leader and for the organization
5	Find and learn from patterns in any quantitative assessment

6	Understand how the survey comments complement the quantitative scores. Don't take them out of context
7	Don't discount bad scores, but try to analyze why they have occurred
8	Share results with the team, clearly explaining what meaningful actions will be taken to improve future scores in the company's weak areas and regularly follow up...
9	...but don't address too many areas for improvement at the same time. Choose one or two keys areas where you can develop clear action plans and show measurable improvement

1. Don't rush into action until you have evaluated the results. Engage the team in this process

2. Avoid getting stuck in analysis paralysis. Turn insights into action

3. Don't take the survey results personally

4. Understand how negative feedback shows opportunities for improvement for you as a leader and for the organization

5. Find and learn from patterns in any quantitative assessment

6. Understand how the survey comments complement the quantitative scores. Don't take them out of context

7. Don't discount bad scores, but try to analyze why they have occurred

8. Share results with the team, clearly explaining what meaningful actions will be taken to improve future scores in the company's weak areas and regularly follow up...

9. ....but don't address too many areas for improvement at the same time. Choose one or two keys areas where you can develop clear action plans and show measurable improvement

KEY TAKEAWAYS

» In a culture of openness, responsibility and honesty, problems don't escalate to become disasters. Learning from mistakes is what makes you and your startup better and stronger every day.
» **Four main elements** form the core of effective, robust communication.
  » **Frequency** relates to how often you communicate with other team members
  » Co-founders have to be **aligned** on any message that goes out
  » Communication has to be **bi-directional** - involve both talking and listening
  » Time for communication needs to be **planned**
» **Four areas to communicate about constantly:**
  » **Values**
  » **Priorities**
  » **Achievements:** Start celebrating every tiny victory!
  » **Failures:** When mistakes happen, be open about them. Failure is the foundation of success
» Give every team member attention. Listen to help you understand what your team needs.
» A culture of giving and providing feedback is key to success.
» **Seven key tips to help you provide meaningful feedback.**
  1) Understand the goal 2) Focus on the issue, not the person 3) Be sensitive about the language used 4) Put your message in writing as well as delivering it verbally 5) Right balance between positive and negative comments 6) Make it one-to-one 7) Clear next steps
» **Six key tips to help you be a good receiver of feedback.**
  1) Reduce your defensiveness
  2) Be curious. Repeat. Ask questions.
  3) Signal understanding
  4) Thank you, thank you, thank you
  5) Know when to stop and when to pause
  6) Respond promptly and be constructive
» **Plan to make feedback an integral part of your startup.**

MENTAL TOUGHNESS

IN THIS CHAPTER, YOU WILL LEARN:

» Why the life of an entrepreneur is like a roller coaster
» What Mental Toughness is
» To understand stress
» How much stress is optimal
» The seven stressors of a founder and how to manage them
» The Mental State Tool
» Leading by example: The mindset of the hero

"AMATEURS SIT AND WAIT FOR INSPIRATION, THE REST OF US JUST GET UP AND GO TO WORK."[141]

- **Stephen King**, *American Author*

---

141 Source: King, S. On Writing: A Memoir of the Craft, Scribner, 2000.

The entrepreneur roller coaster

Mental toughness
The ability to consistently perform toward the upper range of your talent and skill, regardless of competitive circumstances.

If you chose to pick up this book and have read it to this last chapter, you know that being an entrepreneur is not an easy life of riches. It takes hard work and commitment and features a lot of ups and downs.

"Building a startup is like a sadistic rollercoaster...Sometimes you are having fun, and sometimes you are down. But no matter how you feel, you've got to keep going. "
- **Martin Zahuranec**, co-founder & CEO at **eyerim**

As a founder, you're like a firefighter on duty 24/7. Every day, there are both small and big fires to put out. Often, they all break out at the same time. Your top employee resigns, your biggest customer decides to work with someone else, clients delay payments and you don't have enough money to cover the payroll. This is one of the differences between being an entrepreneur and working for a company. You're in command. When a big problem occurs, you and your co-founders have to solve it, even if it's not 'your department'. You own everyone's mistakes.

"I DON'T KNOW ANY STARTUP CEO WHO HAS EVERYTHING PLANNED, WITH NO SURPRISES OCCURRING DURING THE WEEK

OR DAY. SO THERE IS NOTHING TO DO BUT FIGHT THE FIRE AND MAKE SURE THE CAR YOU ARE DRIVING IS PROPERLY BUILT BY THE TIME IT GETS TO THE FINISH LINE AND NO-ONE IS SERIOUSLY HURT."

*- **Kaidi Ruusalepp**, founder & CEO at **Funderbeam** (introduced in the previous chapter)*

Time and patience

Stoyan once took a car sharing service from Aarhus to Copenhagen with the wealthy owner of a Danish company. The company owner was about to retire at the time, but he told Stoyan his story.

He had started the company with two of his friends. They were three co-founders, armed with skills and lots of ambition. They worked very hard for eight years, putting in 12-hour days for six days a week, but were still failing to make the company profitable. They had built a solid team and the revenues were growing, but they were running out of cash. The numbers weren't adding up.

At that point, a large bank made an offer to acquire them. Burned out and exhausted, they almost sold out. Eventually, they decided to turn down the offer and keep going. It was the right move. Within two years, things finally turned around and their financial situation improved. At the time Stoyan met the man, he was already a multimillionaire. It had taken him and the team 10 years of hard work to make the company profitable.

Successful founders are armed with patience. They find a way to fall in love with the process.
They know they will have some good days and many difficult ones. Your ability to deal with stress will be fundamental to your success.

Learning to deal with stress: PicsArt

Hohvannes Avoyan, founder & CEO of PicsArt, whom we met in the Focus & Execution chapter, says stress is part and parcel of the startup experience. "I've learned to adapt to stress, rather than overreacting and treating it like the end of the world," he explains. "I try to recognize that stress is a given and just accept it as quietly and calmly as I can. Failure is part of the game just as much as success, and if you're not ready to fail sometimes, a startup probably isn't the place for you."
No startup will have a straight road to success. "Every company I've founded has had at least one near-death experience, where we lost a major customer or something else happened and I thought it was the end," explains Hovhannes. "After a couple of those experiences, you learn to manage your emotions. You start to recall other times you failed and then things improved, and you realize you'll get through this time, too."

In this chapter, we will explore the concept of mental toughness and why it's important to an entrepreneur.

I TRY TO RECOGNIZE THAT STRESS IS A GIVEN AND JUST ACCEPT IT AS QUIETLY AND CALMLY AS I CAN... FAILURE IS PART OF THE GAME JUST AS MUCH AS SUCCESS, AND IF YOU'RE NOT READY TO FAIL SOMETIMES, A STARTUP PROBABLY ISN'T THE PLACE FOR YOU.

- Hovhannes Avoyan, founder & CEO of PicsArt

What is mental toughness?

Mental toughness is our capacity to deal with stress and challenges. In simple terms, it is the courage to remain calm and move on when 'sh** hits the fan'. It's about how much time you spend focused on the problems and difficulties rather than working on solutions and seeing the bigger picture.

Jim Loehr, a sports psychologist seen by many as a pioneer in the area of mental toughness, defines the concept as *"the ability to consistently perform toward the upper range of your talent and skill, regardless of competitive circumstances."*[142] A discipline first developed in sports, mental toughness has proven to play a significant role in success. For example, a 2003 study[143] by Weinberg and Gould indicated that mental ability contributed over 50% of athletes' success when competing.

Feeling like a winner by doing your utmost: Maria Grozdeva

We reached out to **Maria Grozdeva**, a Bulgarian sport shooter who participated in six Olympic Games, winning two Olympic gold medals. She's the second-best female shooter of all time and Bulgaria's most successful Olympic athlete.

At the 2012 Olympics in London, Maria started shooting with flawless results, scoring 100 out of 100 points. Next, she had two more series of ten shots, each worth 10 points.

Something happened in the last five shots. She was calm and didn't change a thing, but only shot an eight. The next shot she did the same again. She started worrying and checking the cartridges, but it all looked fine. She shot another 10, so she

---

142 Source: Loehr, J.E. The New Toughness Training for Sports, Dutton, 1994.
143 Source: Weinberg, R.S. & Gould, D. Foundations of Sport and Exercise Psychology, Human Kinetics, 2003.

calmed down a bit. But somehow in the last two shots, she only scored eights.

"I felt horrified. I wanted to pack my suitcase and leave. So much training time, deprivation and finally in 40 minutes everything went to hell," she explains. "I had to prepare for the final part of the competition, and I started hearing everyone, from my personal trainer to the gunsmith, encouraging me that I can do it. If I hit only tens (which I'd done hundreds of times at practice). I could enter the final as one of the top eight results," she explains. But she wasn't taking in the encouragement. "I couldn't hear them. I let them speak. I was thinking 'what a loser I am'. As I felt sorry for myself, I heard the gunsmith tell a parable in a trembling voice, with tears in his eyes, as he cleaned my weapon: "The frog got into a bucket of milk. She thought she would never get out, but drown there. Nevertheless, she kept trying to push herself out. As she kept pushing and kicking with her feet, the milk thickened like butter and the frog could get out."

The story gave Maria pause for thought. "It suddenly dawned on me how much these people believed in me, how much they wanted to lift my spirits, while I was sitting there feeling sorry for myself. In fact, I still had a chance. I suddenly felt an uplift of energy and focused to shoot."

Maria thought about nothing but the task at hand and shot 299 out of 300. It was an incredible score.

"When it was over, everyone shouted and applauded from the stands," she explains. "I had done the impossible." But she couldn't relax yet. Maria was in seventh place, but her result was on a par with two others, resulting in a shoot-out between the three of them. Trembling with excitement, she continued.

"I shot a 9 and finished 9th at the Olympics. However, the struggle I had waged lifted me to new heights. I felt like a winner. I believed that nothing was impossible. I believed that with thought and the right attitude one can do anything. In the evening, I celebrated at a restaurant with colleagues and friends, as if I had won another Olympic medal."

You won't always win, but you can maximize your results within the circumstances. It comes down to mastering your mental state, especially when you are under stress.To deal with stress better, we need to understand what it is, how it affects us and what causes it.

Understanding stress

*"**Stress** is the body's reaction to any change that requires an adjustment or response. The body reacts to these changes with physical, mental, and emotional responses."* [144]

THREAT	HORMONE RELEASE	ALERT MODE	BODY RESPONSE
Internal External	Cortisol Adrenaline	Fight Flight	Physical Emotional Mental

Stress is not just a feeling, it's a hard-wired physical response that affects your entire body. In ancient times, stress helped our ancestors survive and deal with threats by keeping them focused and alert. If you didn't react quickly, you could get killed by a bear. Our ancestors were exposed to far bigger dangers than we are. However, our brains haven't evolved to fit our reduced level of immediate threats. We still have similar responses to significantly lesser stressors.

In simple terms, stress works like this: When something happens in the environment - externally or internally - that your brain views as a threat, your brain activates the release of stress hormones such as cortisol and adrenaline to prepare you to deal with it. This puts you

---

144   Source: Cleveland Clinic, What is stress?, n.d.
Retrieved from: https://my.clevelandclinic.org/health/articles/11874-stress

in 'Alert mode', making you ready to face the threat (**fight**) or run away (**flight**). While your focus and ability to execute on one of these options are strong, many other systems in the body shut down. For example, you don't need your immune system, since your body is focused on short-term survival. This body response can be very helpful in the short term, when you are faced with a threat and need to respond urgently. However, if you are exposed to high levels of stress consistently, it can have damaging effects on your health and wellbeing.

The uncertain and dynamic startup environment can be very stressful. Even when faced with seemingly small threats, your body can respond in the same way it would have done thousands of years ago. There's not enough discussion about how much pressure a founder faces. According to a study by Michael Freeman,[145] entrepreneurs are 50% more likely to have mental health conditions such as depression and suicidal thoughts than people who aren't running a company. There are numerous cases of entrepreneurs who take their own lives, often as a consequence of 'business failure', severe depression and hopelessness.

The Optimal Stress Level

THE STRESS CURVE

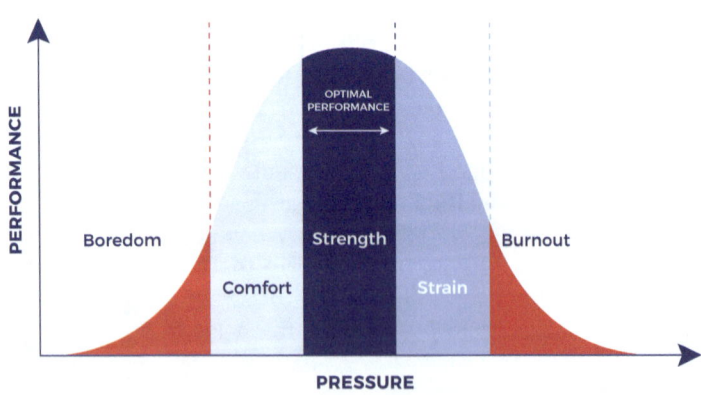

---

145   Source: Freeman, M.A., et al. Are Entrepreneurs "Touches with Fire?, 2015.

Stress is not negative in itself. A certain amount of stress can be positive and even necessary for you to perform at your best. The goal is not to eliminate stress, but instead to learn to co-exist with it, ensuring it doesn't get out of control. Numerous studies, including the work of Yerkes and Dodson[146] as well as Nixon[147] show the correlation between stress and performance. The main finding is that we reach an optimal level of performance when we create a positive level of stress. An example is having a stretch goal or a deadline. Your focus, motivation and overall performance usually increase.

You have to be careful not to expose yourself and your team to very high stress levels consistently, however. These overwhelming levels of stress are what can cause you or your team to burn out.

The seven stressors of a founder

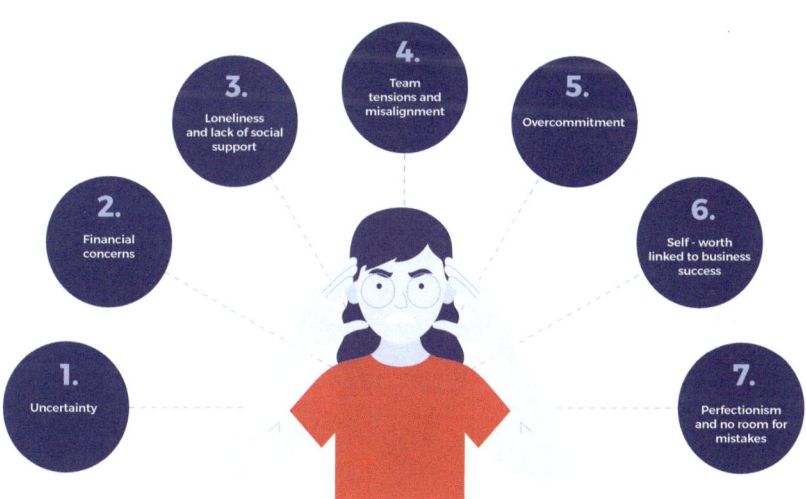

---

146   Source: Yerkes, R.M., & Dodson, J.D. The relation of strength of stimulus to rapidity of habit formation, Journal of Comparative Neurology and Psychology, 1908.
147   Source: Nixon, P. Human Response to Stress Curve, 1979.

1. Uncertainty

Our brains are wired to seek certainty and avoid uncertainty. According to a study[148], a high level of uncertainty activates the amygdala, the emotional center of the brain, which is also triggered by threats or fear. The more uncertainty, the higher the stress level. Being an entrepreneur means you're dealing with high levels of uncertainty.

How to deal with uncertainty

Firstly, accept it at a deep level. Let go of the urge to always have everything under control. Entrepreneurship is a game of chance. Learn to be comfortable with uncertainty. Often you won't have all the answers. You need to be ok with that - nobody does. There will be times when you feel you have too many things 'up in the air'. Trust that everything will be alright and let it go. As Jeff Dance notes in an article for BusinessCollective: *"One of the most common attributes in successful entrepreneurs is enthusiasm for the unknowns."*[149]
Secondly, do what you can to minimize the uncertainties. Make the decisions that need to be made. Have the important conversations and align with people you need to be aligned with.
This book provides many tools to help you and your team get more clarity over what you need to do. Many things are uncertain just because you haven't yet invested the time to organize them. **The Worry Clearing Tool** (below) might also be helpful to you.

2. Financial Concerns

You haven't been an entrepreneur if you haven't faced a financial challenge at some point. Making sure your financials are healthy is one of the core tasks for any founder. Having insufficient funds can be hugely stressful. It can deplete your energy and bring with it feelings of shame, guilt and hopelessness. You need to regain that energy, since

---

148   Source:Hsu, M., et al. Neural System Responding to Degrees of Uncertainty in Human Decision-Making, Science, 2005.
149   Source: Ashoka, How Entrepreneurs Cope With Uncertainty, Forbes, 2012.
      Retrieved from:
      https://www.forbes.com/sites/ashoka/2012/10/23/how-entrepreneurs-cope-with-uncertainty/#3460590e255e

you need it to build and grow your startup.

Don't take financial hardship lightly or underestimate it. There's a long list of startups that were too optimistic, didn't pay enough attention to their financials and folded because they ran out of cash. However, you'll deal with it better if you can keep a cool, calm head.

How to deal with financial concerns

- Learn to be on top of your financials at all times. Make calculations and projections.

- Plan for the worst-case scenario. Have a Plan B if things don't work out as you expect them to. If finance is not one of your strengths, seek mentors that can help you set up a structure around it.

- Prioritise Revenue Generating Activities (RGA). Look at your current list of priorities. Do you spend the right amount of effort to make your startup financially sound?

- Minimize your expenses. Stop spending money on fancy things. Sometimes you may have to work part-time somewhere else, or live in a small apartment with four of your buddies. That's ok. You're building something for the long term.

3. Loneliness & lack of social support

One of the reasons we don't recommend that founders go solo is that it's lonely to be an entrepreneur. Often your friends, your team or your spouse want to support you, but they might not be able to understand what you're going through.

How to deal with loneliness & lack of social support

Make sure you have people around you who you trust and with whom you can share feelings and problems. They could be fellow entrepreneurs or other ambitious professionals.

To develop a network of like-minded people, join a business club or a similar entrepreneurial network. You can also hire a mentor or a coach to support you on the journey. One tool that we strongly recommend is to create your own mastermind group.[150] This is a group of like-minded people who meet on a regular basis, to support each other by openly sharing challenges and successes.

The importance of your peer group:
Degordian

Daniel Ackermann is the co-founder and CEO of Degordian, an independent creative agency based in Croatia, with more than 200 employees. Like many other successful founders, Daniel believes it's important to regularly meet other ambitious entrepreneurs. "Every week I try to meet fellow entrepreneurs of similar size companies," he explains. "Sometimes we meet in a group of four or five and take turns - everyone shares what they currently struggle with and the rest of us offer ideas and advice. Other times I meet people in a one-to-one setup, especially when I need specific advice from someone with experience in an area." Daniel notes that he learns a lot from the meetings. "I feel the benefits of sharing and receiving the support from people on a similar journey to mine" he says.

---

4. Team tensions & misalignment

Misalignment with your team can create a lot of stress. Many founders get very excited about an idea and start a company together before having the important conversations about purpose, values, vision and expectations. They may not even know each other very well. Stoyan recently mentored a founder who was on the brink of burnout. He was working very hard, but his co-founder didn't seem to put in the same level of effort. This scenario can be frustrating and needs to be addressed immediately. Often differences in values, vision or the expected level of commitment can cause companies to fail, despite having skillful and hard-working founders. The more your team grows,

---

150   Mastermind group is a peer-to-peer mentoring format, in which the members help one another to solve their problems through input, advice and accountability.

the greater the likelihood of tensions and misalignment developing between people.

How to deal with tensions and misalignment

In previous chapters, we shared many ideas and tools which help you create initial alignment and prevent some of these problems developing. In essence: **Take your time to choose the right people.** Make sure you always agree on what is expected from you and what you expect from others. As the Marcus Penn character said in the action movie **Under Siege 2:** *"Assumption is the mother of all f***-ups."*[151] As a leader, stay sharp to spot misalignments and address them as early as you can.

5. Overcommitment

Driven by demands, ideas and responsibilities, it's easy for a founder to overcommit and say "yes" to every opportunity. If you're an achiever type, it's likely you have a tendency to overcommit. It's important to be ambitious and to set ambitious goals, but being constantly overwhelmed will do neither you nor your team any good. Too many promises can create excessive expectations, which leads to stress. You may be productive, but if you constantly miss deadlines and targets, you aren't able to appreciate your achievements.

How to deal with overcommitment

In the Focus & Execution chapter, we explored tools and ideas for how to focus on your core priorities. If you're feeling stressed due to overcommitment, it might be a good time to take a step back and reassess. Here are a few helpful questions for reflection:

- Is this just an intense period or has it felt this way for months and years?

- Which projects and responsibilities can you let go or delegate?

- What can you do to become better at saying "no" and promising less?

---

151   Source: Murphy, G., dir., Under Siege Dark Territory (1995; Burbank, CA; Distributed by Warner Home Video, 2008, Bluray Video).

Talk to your team and share how you feel. Involve the team in helping you come up with solutions.

6. Linking self-worth to business success

As a founder, you spend long hours working on your company. It's very hard not to get attached to it and to link your self-worth to the results you produce. Since it's important to care for your business and be committed to it, it's very easy to take this too far and take it too much to heart.

Things won't always go to plan. You'll make mistakes and some of them will be significant. This doesn't make you worth less as a person and an individual.

How to deal with the problem of linking your self-worth to business success

Have a life outside your startup. Your startup is a very important area of focus, but it's not the only one. Make sure you prioritize time for things that matter to you: friends, relationships and social life. This will help you disconnect from work and gain perspective.

Expand your horizons by reading books, listening to podcasts and watching videos on business and personal development. Perhaps experiment with journaling.

If you've had a long day and you can't get your business worries out of your head, allow yourself to take it easy.

When feeling overwhelmed, Stoyan, for example, likes to slow down and watch a movie from the Marvel Cinematic Universe. It shifts his focus away from work and helps him come back fresher.

7. Perfectionism and no room for mistakes

Perfectionism can have negative effects on your performance as well as your mental health. Perfectionism, broadly defined as "a combination of excessively high personal standards and overly critical self-evaluations" is a huge stress creator. When you believe everything you're doing should be perfect, you become reluctant to complete a task. You're afraid to deliver unless it reaches the unreasonably high standards you set.

How to deal with perfectionism

As explored in the chapter on Focus & Execution, you have to learn to Let it go. A few of the founders interviewed for this book shared the same mindset: "Done is better than perfect".
If you've been struggling with perfectionism for a long time, it might take time to develop the non-perfectionist muscle. Commit to being an entrepreneur and not a perfectionist. Pick your battles and do your very best with the things that matter most.

Have an honest look at these stressors. Which one do you struggle with most?
Which one needs immediate attention?

Exercise: Worry Clearing Tool

This useful exercise helps you clarify what stresses you and what you can do about it. You can do it individually or with your team. Do it the next time you're feeling stressed.
Stress often comes from uncertainty, so bringing clarity to the situation is paramount. Do this by breaking things down and acting accordingly.

Step 1: Make a list of the things that worry you the most
What do you worry most about? What keeps you up at night? Write it down
A list may look like this:

Will we get funding before we run out of cash?
Can I deliver on all these commitments?
Not enough time for friends and social life
Covid-19 pandemic

Step 2: Look at your list and place things in two columns **Things I can control** and **Things I can't control:**

Things I can control	Things I can't control
Will we find funding before we run out of cash?	Covid-19 pandemic
Can I deliver on all these commitments?	
Not enough time for friends and social life	

Step 3: Measure the impact

How much does each of these worries affect you on a scale from 1 to 10?

Things I can control	Things I can't control
[8] Will we find funding before we run out of cash?	[9] Covid-19 pandemic
[3] Can I deliver on all these commitments?	
[6] Not enough time for friends and social life	

Step 4: Get specific and create solutions

For the things you can control:

- Come up with concrete ideas and solutions

How can you solve this challenge? And if you don't have the answers, can you ask someone for advice?

For example:

[8] Will we find funding before we run out of cash?

- Meet financial advisor and generate ideas

- Start aggressively implementing the sales strategy

- Build a Plan B if investment doesn't go through

For the Things you can't control:

• Ask yourself:

How can you see it differently? How can you find a new perspective?
Often stress occurs because of a feeling of helplessness or hopelessness. For things you **can't** control, consider and try to understand that it doesn't make rational sense to spend much time worrying about it. Why worry if it's beyond your control?
Could you find an opportunity coming out of it, or a better perspective? For example:

[9] Covid-19 pandemic

• More time to build the product

• Lots of talent might be laid off. We can hire great people

• Great opportunity to restructure our business model

• New challenges for the business world, which we can solve to generate new revenue

Mastering your mental state

To be a successful founder and leader of a team, it's important to take control of your mental state; to retain a cool head despite external events and circumstances. Just like Ivaylo Petrov - Sensei (5th Dan Black Belt Aikido[152] Master) recommends: "You have to be able to create space between yourself and the problem you're facing. Otherwise you can get absorbed by it and you have no chance to react appropriately."

---

152   Aikido is a system derived from the martial traditions of Japan. It is a special kind of martial art that stesses spiritual development.

Your mental toughness will be challenged in a variety of situations. There will be days when you need to remind yourself that some things are outside your control. As an entrepreneur, you will face numerous unexpected and uncomfortable situations. Whatever happens, it's your responsibility to stay calm, take ownership of the situation and move forward.

Take a breath and focus on solving the problem: phyre

The CEO of phyre, **Konstantin Djelebov**, who you met in the chapter on Robust Communication, knows that no matter how much you plan, unexpected things might occur.

One Saturday, he was making his morning coffee. He was excited, looking forward to Monday's launch of a national campaign by his biggest client to date. The client would be using phyre's product. Suddenly, he received multiple messages from his team's slack account. There was an outage, the system was failing and the team couldn't figure out what the problem was. The customer was contacting his team in panic. While Konstantin looked at the problem, his mom called to say she wasn't feeling well and needed to go to the hospital. On top of that, his electricity blew up.

Konstantin has learned from experience that the best thing to do in such instances is to calm down, **shut everything down and focus on solving the problem.** He took a deep breath and **made a list** of the most **urgent** next steps. First, he arranged a hospital visit for his mom, then he called his provider to solve the electricity issue.

From then on, he could focus fully on resolving the issue. Konstantin knew that calming the situation down was first priority. He called the client, informed him personally about the situation and assured him that regular updates would follow. The client was very understanding. Konstantin then connected with his senior team, creating a plan of action. He removed a person who was spreading negative energy to the team. He wasn't needed at that moment. Finally, he cut all external communication to the team that was solving the issue. It only created additional tension and didn't help. With a calmer environment, the team got to work. It turned out the problem was connected to an external server, unrelated to their product. After what felt like a very long weekend, the issue was successfully resolved. When Monday came, not only did the campaign run smoothly. Konstantin had built a better relationship with his client. They knew that he would have their back, even if things got out of control.

The Mental State Tool

The first step towards helping us improve our mental state is to understand it. The Mental State Tool can help you. It's inspired by founder of **iPEC Coaching**[153], **Bruce Schneider's** Self-Perception Chart, from his book Energy Leadership: *Transforming your Workplace and Your Life from the Core.*[154]

More than anything, it's an awareness tool. It has helped Stoyan and hundreds of startup founders to master their mental game and understand their teams better.

THE MENTAL STATE TOOL

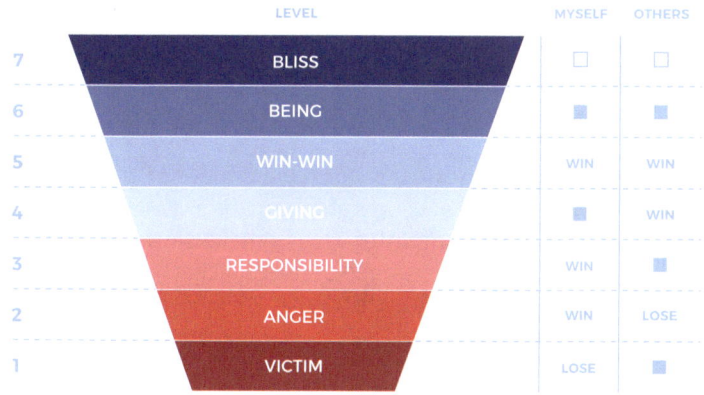

---

153   iPEC coaching is one of the largest ICF certified coach training schools in the world with over 10,000 graduates.
154   Source: Schneider, B. D. Energy Leadership: Transforming your Workplace and Your Life from the Core, Wiley, 2007.

Level 1 - Victim
The lowest level is Victim. At that level you feel sorry for yourself. You're immersed in your own problems, you feel stuck and your vision is narrow. You feel like whatever you do **you** will **lose**. There's no solution, only hopelessness. At this level, taking action doesn't come naturally. Your focus is so much on your own problems that you can't think of others. It's all about yourself and you feel hopeless.

Level 2 - Anger
Level 2 is associated with Anger. At this level your focus is to **win** at the expense of an opposing side. It's all black and white. You're right and they're wrong. You win and they lose.
The positive side to Level 2 compared to Level 1 is that you want to take action. However, this is still a very ego-driven level. You're not able to make rational choices. It's all about 'proving the other side wrong'.

Level 3 - Responsibility
At Level 3, you start acknowledging others. Achieving your goal is still what matters most to you, but it's ok for others to **win**, too, as long as their actions don't affect you. You have to win at all costs, but **if others win, it's fine by you**. At this level, you start taking a wider perspective.
As a movie producer on set, Stoyan often operated at level 3 during production. He had to take control because as a producer. His role was to make sure the team got all the shots they needed. Time and speed were of major importance. There wasn't much time for emotions and explanations. Stoyan's sole purpose was to ensure the team got the highest quality material for the client. Given the tight shooting schedules, the team was also aware of this need.

Level 4 - Giving
Level 4 is giving. When you operate from this state, it's all about **another** person or people. Your focus is to make sure **they win**. If you also benefit from the situation, even better, but that's not your focus. If you help someone out without expecting anything in return, you may be operating from Level 4.

Level 5 - Win-Win
Level 5 is the most entrepreneurial state. That's the level in which you

find opportunities even if the circumstances seem negative. The world is abundant and anything that happens fuels ideas for how to create a win-win situation. If a client postpones a meeting for a new project and your reaction is: *'Great, we can do it next week and have more time for the other projects,'* you're probably operating from Level 5.

Level 6 – Being
Level 6 is the mental state in which you are fully present and almost non-judgemental. Things are what they are and everything happens for a reason. In this state, it doesn't matter who wins or loses. You are letting go and just enjoying what life offers.

Level 7 – Bliss
The place of absolute happiness. You are one with everything and completely aligned. This is the level at which you're 'in the moment'. It's the highest state of consciousness and the peak mental state, a place where your awareness is greatly expanded.

When using this tool, your goal is to identify which state you are in at the moment and consciously decide what level would be most appropriate for the situation. It aims to create space between you and your emotions.

For example, if a client sends you an angry email, what's your first reaction? Do you want to write back and show them they're wrong? (Level 2). **Before you act, ask yourself whether that is the most productive way to deal with the situation.**

Sometimes, when you're feeling very low (Level 1 or 2), you can ask yourself "How would I react if I was operating from a higher mental state (say, Level 5)? What can I do to lift myself up?" Maybe you should go for a walk or listen to a favourite song, or call a friend or a mentor? Once you're higher up the ladder, your chances of making a productive decision increase.

It is important to note that every level has its place and time. None of them is negative as such. When you raise your mental state, you're more likely to consciously decide on the best level to operate from.

What do you do that gets you to a higher mental state?

The Mental State Tool can be very useful in understanding members of your team and helping them perform better as well. If you know your co-founder had a bad day and dropped to Level 1, you can be empathetic and find a way to lift them up. Sometimes, they might need some support (Level 4), or a little tough love (Level 2), to stop feeling like a victim and start taking action.

We recommend Bruce Schender's book *Energy Leadership: Transforming your Workplace and Your Life from the Core*, filled with practical examples of how to apply the mental state tool.

Leading by example: the mindset of the hero

"WHEN THERE IS DANGER, A GOOD LEADER TAKES THE FRONT LINE. BUT WHEN THERE IS CELEBRATION, A GOOD LEADER STAYS IN THE BACK ROOM."[155]

- **Nelson Mandela**, *Former President of South Africa*

---

[155] Source: Oprah.com. Oprah Talks to Nelson Mandela, n.d. Retrieved from: https://www.oprah.com/world/oprah-interviews-nelson-mandela/6#

Do you have the drive to be the very best every day, even when you're having a bad day? Your role as a leader is not just to perform, it's to encourage everyone around you to grow and build a team that can do something impressive in the long run. To do that well, you need to become a master of your mental state, especially in critical situations.

One way to help you do this is to start seeing yourself in the role of the hero. As a movie producer, Stoyan has always been fascinated by stories and how they are created. Since ancient times, humans have told stories of heroes embarking on exciting and unbelievable adventures, to return with or without a reward, but certainly growing as people. Movies tell those same stories now.

Entrepreneurship is just like those hero stories and movies. It's filled with ups and downs. You're on a quest to achieve an ambitious vision against difficult odds. By default, that means you will get hit and tested many times. Every time you have a setback, you can choose how to show up:

1. As the hero of the story

Heroes make mistakes. But when mistakes happen, they take full ownership of what's happened and move on fast. They see the setbacks and obstacles as a normal part of the journey and try to turn them into stepping stones for their future success. They know that every minute of whining, complaining and negative energy is time that can be invested in solving and creating new opportunities. They are **proactive** and shape their own reality.

2. As the victim of the story

Victims focus on blaming external circumstances and events. They always believe that someone or something else is responsible for their problems and mistakes. Victims have a hard time getting over failures and moving on. They struggle to see the long-term perspective. They are **reactive.**

Think about the last few times you had a setback. In what proportion of those instances did you act as a **Hero vs Victim**? What can you do to improve your score?

Deal from strength: Mark Harrison from The T1 Agency

You already met **Mark Harrison,** founder & CEO of The T1 Agency, in the Effective Planning chapter. He learned a trick to help his mental state in his 20s: "When I was at a meeting and somebody was yelling at me or I wasn't succeeding… I would take a pen and I would just write on a piece of paper the letters D.F.S. And that was a mental trigger for me. It meant Deal From Strength. Because when you don't deal from strength you are in trouble. And that little trigger I use to this day allows me to get to a comfort zone. When you get a hit: Don't feel weak, don't panic, don't be alarmed. Just deal from strength."

Sometimes you will be overwhelmed, stressed and exhausted, but your team members need you to lead them and give them direction through difficult times as well. Even if you don't have all the answers, you need to take ownership and take care of the team.

A great example of this is Marian Temelkov, founder and Global CEO of Dynamis Group. He was running a company with a co-founder, but Marian felt their views and vision weren't compatible. In 2019, a settlement was reached for Marian to be able to continue operating with a new business in the same industry and keep his team.

In order to finance the settlement, he had to borrow a significant sum of money, which meant that the new company started out saddled with debt. The next six months were very difficult. The team was working from coffee shops, or any place they could find. Marian worked all waking hours, including weekends and late nights. While going through all the stress, he managed to keep his team motivated and inspired. Even in the hardest moments, he would remain positive and calm and not let his team lose courage.

At times it felt like mission impossible, but Marian kept going. The effort finally paid off. With incredible commitment and execution, Marian managed not only to pay back the full amount in less than six months, but also to open a new office in Sofia and hire five new people.

"The right thing to do is to never leave your team behind," Marian says.

"AS A CEO, THE ONLY WAY TO GO THROUGH STRUGGLES WHEN WORKING WITH A TEAM IS TO SHIELD THEM, TO TAKE FULL RESPONSIBILITY AND COSTS, TO COVER THEM. IT WASN'T EVEN A CHOICE FOR ME IN THIS SITUATION. I WOULD FIGHT WITH ANYTHING I HAVE TO KEEP THEM

AND MAKE THEM FEEL SAFE. FORTUNATELY, IT WORKED WELL IN THE END, AND ALL BUT TWO EMPLOYEES ARE STILL PART OF THE TEAM TO THIS DAY."

- Marian Temelkov, Founder & Global CEO of Dynamis Group

In stressful situations, you need to be at the frontline and **lead by example**. As a founder, you are the leader of your company and your team will base its actions on your behaviour and mindset. They are watching how you act. You can't expect your team to do something if you're not ready to do it yourself.

Join the troops: Kai Schukowski from Grand Hotel Kempinski Vilnius

Kai Schukowski is the general manager (GM) of Grand Hotel Kempinski Vilnius and the youngest GM in the history of Kempinski Hotels. Since he became GM, the hotel has won numerous awards for hospitality in the region.

He says that when employees are overwhelmed, he makes sure he's personally in the hotel to help everyone. "As a leader, you need to leave your ego at the door. If I am not able to go and help out the dishwashers when they are overwhelmed, or support the housekeepers in tidying up the rooms, then how can I expect them to do the same? At the end of the day, we are all one team, we fight for the same mission and we need to support each other, especially in times of pressure."

KEY TAKEAWAYS

» **Entrepreneurship is like a roller coaster** and you need to have the ability to deal with daily problems and stress.

» **Mental Toughness** is " the ability to consistently perform toward the upper range of your talent and skill regardless of competitive circumstances." It's a skill that can be developed to give you an edge in your entrepreneurial journey.

» **Stress** is the body's reaction to any change that requires an adjustment or response.

» A limited amount of stress can improve performance, but excessive stress is harmful in the long term.

» **The 7 Stressors of a founder are:**

» 1) Uncertainty 2) Financial concerns 3) Loneliness & social support 4) Team tensions & misalignment 5) Overcommitment 6) Self-worth linked to business success 7) Perfectionism and no room for mistakes

» **Understanding and managing your mental state** will not only help you be a better founder, but also a better leader of your team. **The Mental State Tool** can help you.

» The best founders **don't let the circumstances define their results.** They envision the future and create opportunities even in times of struggle. When times get tough, they step in and protect their teams.

Afterword

So here you are at the end of the book. But is that the end? Not nearly. It's merely the beginning of your journey. The journey of building a sustainable company with a strong focus on culture, performance and leadership.

All the tools, principles and ideas covered in this book are not to be seen just as a knowledge -these are to be applied consistently. Only then the results are likely to follow.

To help you stay on track - let us introduce you to **The PERFORM Assessment tool.** Apply it by simply measuring each area from PERFORM from 1 to 10 or by filling in the boxes.

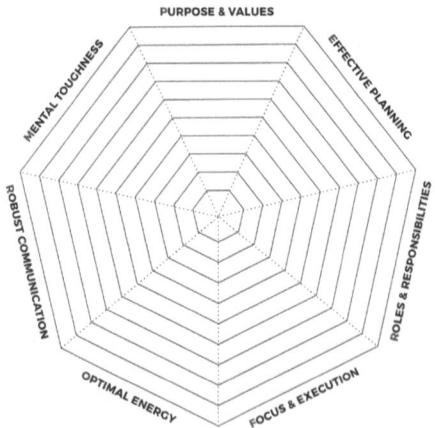

Let everyone from the team assess each area in private first. Share and discuss the results together. Compare your numbers and find out why there are differences in your perceptions. See which areas need your attention and commit to make the necessary improvements.

Nothing will ever be perfect. But with consistency and commitment you have a chance to build a meaningful company with a team that will make all hardships be worth it during the journey and at the end of it.

Thank you for your attention, commitment and GO PERFORM!
Cristobal and Stoyan

Next steps

We hope to stay connected.
Here are several ways you can get in touch with the authors and their projects.

The PERFORM movement
performnow.eu
Join for free resources and additional materials.

Startup Wise Guys
www.startupwiseguys.com
Check out the programs of the leading B2B accelerator in Europe.

Stoyan Yankov
www.stoyanyankov.com
Get in touch with Stoyan for a personalized team workshop or individual coaching session.

The authors

Stoyan Nikolaev Yankov

Stoyan Yankov is a productivity & performance coach and a global keynote speaker. Stoyan specializes in coaching founders and entrepreneurs, and since 2015 has helped over 200 teams grow as individuals and create more productive and mindful company cultures. Stoyan began his entrepreneurial career in 2011 and has a background in video and movie production, creating premium event experiences, and building global business networks. Today, Stoyan shares advice on productivity and performance through keynotes, workshops and bootcamps in over 25 countries, sharing the stage with some of the most influential thought leaders, such as David Allen, Guy Kawasaki, Salim Ismail and Deepak Chopra. He is also a managing partner at Samodiva Masterminds, a company focused on exclusive mastermind experiences and corporate offsite, as well as the host of the Productivity Mastery podcast. He holds an MSc degree in Finance from Aarhus University - BSS.

Jose Cristobal Alonso Martin

Cristobal Alonso is the definition of a global CEO. He is an experienced serial entrepreneur, 3 time CEO, a serial early-stage investor with more than 150 investments, and a global executive who has led teams and projects up to 500 people. He has lived and worked in 5 continents, 20+ countries and 36 cities. Cristobal is CEO and "El Patron" of Startup Wise Guys, the most experienced B2B accelerator in Europe, investing in early stage SaaS, sustainability, cyber security and fintech B2B startups. He is passionate about coaching startups on purpose & culture as well as funding and pitch training. Cristobal has extensive experience as the public face of media outreach campaigns and is a frequent keynote speaker at webinars, startup and Telco conferences, and panels around the world. He holds an MBA from INSEAD and serves as President of the INSEAD's Global Entrepreneurship Club and the Spanish INSEAD Alumni Association. Cristobal is also a former professional basketball player, enjoys playing the piano, and sharing his love for cooking and wine with as many guests as possible.

Acknowledgements

We would like to thank everyone who has contributed for making this book happen!

Special thanks to all founders & other professionals who were generous enough to share their learnings:

[in Alphabetical Order]

Alexander Zlatkov 🏴, CEO & Co-founder of SessionStack 🏴, https://www.sessionstack.com/

Anders Thomsen 🇩🇰, CEO & Co-founder of no-more 🇩🇰, https://nomorehours.com/

Andrey Khusid 🏴, CEO & Co-founder of Miro 🏴, https://miro.com/

Andrew Tarvin 🇺🇸, CEO & Founder of Humour That Works 🇺🇸, https://www.humorthatworks.com/

Anna Andersone 🏴, CEO & Founder of be-with 🏴, https://bewithclothing.com/

Anna Stepanoff 🏴, CEO & Co-founder of Wild Code School 🇫🇷, https://www.wildcodeschool.com/

Artis Kehris 🏴, COO & Co-founder of Printify 🏴, https://printify.com/

Ashot Tonoyan 🏴, Managing Director at ServiceTitan 🏴, https://www.servicetitan.com/

Boris Borisov 🏴, COO & Co-founder of RemoteMore 🏴, https://remotemore.com/

Boris Krastev 🏴, CEO & Co-founder of RemoteMore 🏴

Claus Fraussing Nielsen 🇩🇰, CEO & Founder of Talium Accounting 🇩🇰 https://talium.dk/

Daniel Ackerman 🏴, CEO & Co-founder of Degordian 🏴, https://degordian.com/

Daria Dubinina 🇺🇦, CEO & Co-founder of Crassula 🏴, https://crassula.io/

Daumantas Dvilinskas 🏴, CEO & Co-founder of TransferGo 🏴, https://www.transfergo.com/

David Allen 🇺🇸, CEO & Founder of GTD Methodology 🇺🇸, https://gettingthingsdone.com/

Dillon Hall 🇺🇸, CEO (Europe) & Co-founder of Simporter 🏴,

Frederikke Schmidt 🇩🇰, CEO & Founder of roccamore 🇩🇰, https://roccamore.eu/

Hedi Mardisoo 🏴, CEO & Co-founder of Cachet 🏴, https://cachet.me/

Hovhannes Avoyan 🏴, CEO & Founder of PicsArt 🏴, https://picsart.com/

Ilma Nausedaite 🏴, COO & Co-founder of MailerLite 🏴, https://www.mailerlite.com/

Iva Tsolova 🏴, CEO & Co-founder of JAMBA 🏴, https://jamba.bg/

Ivaylo Petrov - Sensei 🏴, Founder of Aikischool 🏴, https://aikischoolbg.com/

Jeff Lawson 🇺🇸, CEO & Co-founder of Twilio 🇺🇸, https://www.twilio.com/

Johanna Mai-Riisma 🇪🇪, CEO & Co-founder of Zelos 🇪🇪, https://www.getzelos.com/

Kai Schukowski 🇩🇪, General Manager at Grand Hotel Kempinski 🇧🇬, https://www.kempinski.com/

Kaidi Ruusalep 🇪🇪, CEO & Founder of Funderbeam 🇪🇪, https://www.funderbeam.com/

Konstantin Djelebov 🇧🇬, CEO & Co-founder of phyre 🇧🇬, https://www.phyreapp.com/

Kubilay Onur Gungor 🇹🇷, CEO & Co-founder of Cyber Struggle 🇪🇪, https://cyberstruggle.org/

Laimonas Noreika 🇱🇹, CEO & Co-founder of ZITICITY 🇱🇹, https://ziticity.com

Mansukh Patel 🇮🇳, Founder of DruYoga 🇬🇧, https://druyoga.com/

Margarita Sivakova 🇧🇬, CEO & Co-founder of Legal Nodes 🇬🇧, https://legalnodes.org/

Marian Temelkov 🇧🇬, CEO & Founder of Dynamis Group 🇬🇧 ,https://www.dynamisconsultancy.com/

Maris Dagis 🇱🇻, CEO & Co-founder of Sellfy 🇱🇻,https://sellfy.com/

Mariya Grozdeva 🇧🇬, 2x Olympic Gold Medalist in Pistol Shooting

Mark Harrison 🇨🇦, CEO & Founder of The T1 Agency 🇨🇦, https://thet1agency.com/

Martin Varēs 🇪🇪, CEO & Co-founder of Fractory 🇪🇪, https://fractory.com/

Martin Zahuranec 🇸🇰, CEO & Co-founder of Eyerim 🇸🇰, https://www.eyerim.com/

Melissa Rosenthal 🇺🇸, CEO & Co-founder of Circle 🇺🇸, https://www.circletxt.com/

Mette Lykke 🇩🇰, CEO of Too Good to Go 🇩🇰, https://toogoodtogo.org/

Mindaugas Mozuras 🇱🇹, Head of Engineering at Vinted 🇱🇹, https://www.vinted.com/

Oliver Gasser 🇨🇭 CEO & Co-founder of Moduulo 🇪🇪

Radha Patel 🇬🇧, Founder of Toga 🇬🇧, https://www.togaonline.co.uk/

Roberts Bernans 🇱🇻, CPO & Co-founder of Nordigen 🇱🇻, https://nordigen.com/

Sergiu Negut 🇷🇴, EVP & Co-founder of Fintech OS 🇬🇧, https://fintechos.com/

Steli Efti 🇬🇷, CEO & Co-founder of Close.com 🇺🇸, https://close.com/

Tatsiana Zaretskaya 🇧🇾, CEO & Founder of Laava Tech 🇪🇪, https://laavatech.com/

Thibaut Taittinger 🇫🇷, CEO & Founder of Puzl CowOrKing 🇧🇬, https://www.puzl.com/

Thomas Midtgaard Jorgensen 🇩🇰, CEO & Co-founder of Rocket57 🇩🇰

Viktoriya Vasilenko 🇺🇸, CEO & Founder of Knowledge Gate Group 🇩🇰,
https://www.knowledgegategroup.com/

Vlad Larin 🇲🇩, Co-founder of Zeroqode 🇲🇩, https://zeroqode.com/

Zsolt Kelliar 🇭🇺, CEO & Co-founder of Talentuno 🇭🇺, https://talentuno.com/

We've also included examples from:

Anthony Robbins, Bruce Lee, Doc Rivers, Eric Edmeades, Jack Zenger & Joe Folkman, Jennifer Petriglieri, Kalman Victor, Josiah Charles Stamp, Mark Sanborn, Nelson Mandela, Peter Drucker, Nassim Nicholas Taleb, Ray Dalio, Simon Sinek, Tony Hsieh, Michael Freeman, Elbruz Yilmaz, Mick Lubinskas, Phil Jackson, James C. Humes, Jim Loehr, Marcus Buckingham and Ashley Goodall.

Special thanks

We would like to thank everyone who helped us to make this book come to life.

Thank you to our editor **Jessica Sandin** for the incredible commitment to lift our standards up, providing us with the necessary "tough love" within a few rounds of feedback and for improving the language style.

Thank you to our designer **Agne Strimaityte** for creating the visual style, all the graphics and the layout of the book.

Thank you to **Marija Gracova** for the multiple proof-reading rounds and all important admin work around the book.

Thank you also everyone else who contributed to the book in one way or another by providing feedback, sharing advice, helping us to set up interviews with the founders and last but not least supporting us to keep going and making a better book.

Zane Bojare, Sandro Bortesi, Annija Matisone, Andrey Iliev, Razvan Suta, Justina Ribaviciute, Uldis Zeidurs, Georgi Temelkov, Veselin Tonov, Else Källo, Dimitar Cholakov, Slav Iliev, Eli Draganova, Brianna Quintero, Jurate Puodziukaite, Marge Maidla, Ilona Beliatskaya, Alona Belinska, Rimma Perelmuter, Goda Juskeviciute, Gunce Onur, Cosmin Pirvu, Andrea Mazgaleva.

And if for some reason we forgot to mention you, make sure to let us know, so we will include you in the next edition of the book.

Made in the USA
Columbia, SC
15 February 2024